A YEARBOOK OF
BUDDHIST
WISDOM

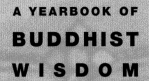

IN SPRING HUNDREDS OF FLOWERS;
IN AUTUMN A HARVEST MOON;
IN SUMMER A REFRESHING BREEZE;
IN WINTER SNOW WILL ACCOMPANY YOU.
IF USELESS THINGS DO NOT HANG IN YOUR MIND,
ANY SEASON IS A GOOD SEASON FOR YOU.

PAUL REPS (COMP.)

Zen Flesh, Zen Bones

A YEARBOOK OF

BUDDHIST

WISDOM

NORMA LEVINE

QUEST BOOKS
THE THEOSOPHICAL PUBLISHING HOUSE

WHEATON, IL U.S.A. / MADRAS, INDIA

For additional information write to

QUEST BOOKS
The Theosophical Publishing House
P.O. Box 270
Wheaton, IL 60189–0270

A publication of the Theosophical Publishing House,
a department of the Theosophical Society in America.

This publication was made possible with the assistance of the Kern Foundation.

DESIGNED AND PRODUCED BY THE BRIDGEWATER BOOK COMPANY LIMITED

Library of Congress Cataloging-in-Publication Data

Levine, Norma, 1943-
        A yearbook of Buddhist wisdom/Norma Levine
        p. cm.
        "Quest books."
        ISBN 0–8356–0743–7
        1. Buddhist devotional calendars. 2. Buddhist meditations.
    I. Title
    BQ5580.L48 1996
    294.3'443--dc20   95-46703
                                                                         CIP

Printed and bound in Hong Kong

CONTENTS

HOW TO USE THIS BOOK

A Yearbook of Buddhist Wisdom follows the four seasons, spring, summer, autumn, and winter, giving philosophical insights attuned to the natural cycle of awakening, blossoming, fruition, and tranquility. The seasonal periods in the book start with March as the first month of spring following the traditional *roman calendar* of the northern hemisphere.

Most Buddhist traditions follow a *lunar calendar*. In the Tibetan tradition six special meditation days occur each month. These, together with the festival days of the Buddha and other important anniversaries of great sages, are related to the cycle of the moon which is never the same year to year.

There are four phases of the moon: the *new moon* which is followed by the *waxing quarter moon* approximately seven days later, which in turn is followed by the *full moon* approximately seven days after that, with the *waning quarter moon* again approximately seven days later, and then returning to a new cycle with the new moon. This cycle takes place over 28, 29, or 30 days, and there are twelve lunar months in a year.

A Yearbook of Buddhist Wisdom follows the lunar calendar according to the Tibetan Buddhist tradition in which the date of the first lunar day of the first lunar month (or New Year) moves between the New Moon in February and the New Moon in March and is determined each year by astrologers in northern India. The days of each month are numbered from 1 to 30 with the full moon falling on the fifteenth day of the month and the new moon on the thirtieth. To achieve this 30-day cycle, some days are doubled up and others are dropped.

Some Buddhist traditions, including the Zen tradition, follow the roman or solar calendar used in the West, and anniversaries celebrated in the Soto Zen tradition are given their roman calendar dates in this *Yearbook*.

LUNAR CYCLE

NEW MOON

☽ WAXING QUARTER MOON

◯ FULL MOON

☾ WANING QUARTER MOON

DIAGRAM OF LUNAR CYCLE

Each Buddhist day in *A Yearbook of Buddhist Wisdom* is given either its lunar or roman date. To place the Buddhist dates from the lunar calendar onto the roman calendar, first consult a roman calendar which gives the phases of the moon – most calendars show this.

You then need to determine the date of the Tibetan New Year – first day of the first lunar month – by contacting a Tibetan Buddhist center.

From the date of the New Year, you will then be able to count forward 13, 14 or 15 days depending on the natural length of the lunar cycle to find the next full moon on which *Full Moon Day* is observed in the Tibetan tradition – the fifteenth day of the month.

The other meditation days, festival days, and anniversaries then fall between these dates each month – for example, *Medicine Buddha Day* always occurs on the eighth day of the month.

The six **Meditation Days** for each season give invocations to awaken inherent wisdom. These days occur on the same day of each lunar month.

Introduction to each season explains the Buddhist view of the passage of the season. Teachings from ancient masters of all Buddhist traditions are woven with occasional poems from contemporary teachers to show the timeless currency of Buddhist wisdom.

There are many great sages who are significant within the Buddhist tradition whose **Anniversaries** of birth or death are marked throughout the year.

There are four **Festival Days** of the Buddha which are celebrated in particular seasons of the year.

INTRODUCTION

The central event of the Buddhist year is the full moon of late spring, when the Buddha attained enlightenment and subsequently passed into pari-nirvana – the name for the death of an enlightened one. From this heroic achievement radiate the special days in the Buddhist calendar: observance of the new moon, full moon, and quarter moon. Equally from the Buddha's teaching comes the enlightenment of the Tibetan yogis such as Milarepa, Zen masters such as Bodhidharma, and spiritual leaders such as the Dalai Lama. The observance of their anniversaries – either birth or death – marks the passage of the Buddhist year.

The goal of Buddhism is the attainment of nirvana – a state of nonduality outside the wheel of cyclic existence, or samsara. In Tibetan Buddhist iconography, samsara is depicted as a circle divided into six realms, gripped in the jaws of a fierce black demon known as Yama, the Lord of Time. Inside the circle of time, there is pleasure and pain. Outside it are the Buddhas who dwell in the bliss of present awareness. Paradoxically, the Buddhist calendar celebrates the attainments of those who have gone beyond the divisions of time.

Cutting through the cycle of existence is the purpose of life. Thus, there are few special days set aside for commemorating peasants' festivals, workers' triumphs, political events, or battle victories. Why celebrate transient glories when the Buddha has shown them to be no more than the upward curve of a cycle of suffering?

The full moon day of the Buddha's enlightenment sets the rhythm of the Buddhist year in a lunar cycle, following the tradition of Indian astrology at the time of his birth. The Tibetan tradition is particularly adept in using the energy of the lunar cycle to assist meditators to achieve harmony with the natural current of the cosmos. There are six special meditation days a month, each with its own type of energy. Medicine Buddha Day is the eighth day of the month; Padmasambhava Day is the tenth; Full Moon Day is the fifteenth; Dakini (goddess) Day is the twenty-fifth; Protector Day is the twenty-ninth; and New Moon Day is the thirtieth. In terms of energies, these correspond to growth, healing power, transformation, fullness, female wisdom, and wrathfulness. On each of these days there are appropriate meditative invocations to awaken inherent wisdom.

Right time, right place brings about auspicious coincidence. The completeness of the full moon enhanced the radiance of the Buddha's mind, signifying its perfection. He became enlightened outside, under a bodhi tree. He also died, or attained parinirvana, on the same full moon day nearly fifty years later, lying on his side on the ground, facing north, under the falling blossoms of a sal tree.

While the eighth day of the quarter moon is observed by all Buddhists — as are the new and full moon days — it has a particular significance in Tibetan Buddhism. The eighth day is known as Medicine Buddha Day and corresponds to the time when Lord Buddha transformed himself into a blue healing Buddha to deliver the Medical Tantras, the basis of the Tibetan medical tradition. On this day the healing energy of the Medicine Buddha, if invoked, is more powerful. According to Buddhist teachings, illness is often an imbalance of the elements — earth, fire, water, wind, and space — manifesting in the body as a result of a tight mental attitude. Ego-fixation induces loneliness, grasping, and anxiety — all causes of illness. Special prayers to the Medicine Buddha invoke the

The Buddha
ODILON REDON 1840–1916

healing power of light rays to purify and open the chakras so that neurotic patterns unknot.

The tenth day of the lunar month celebrates miraculous transformation. Padmasambhava, the Tantric Buddha of Tibet (also known as Guru Rinpoche or Precious Teacher), was born miraculously 12 years after the Buddha's passing from a lotus on a lake in the Swat Valley of what is now Pakistan. His supernatural life, which spanned thirteen hundred years right into eighth-century Tibet, is an epic drama of transformation. Padmasambhava spontaneously demonstrated the Tantric path to the deluded. For example, April commemorates the time when the king of Zahor in India tried to burn him alive because he suspected an illicit love affair with his daughter, the princess Mandarava. Padmasambhava transformed the fire into a lake, and the king beheld him sitting in the center in Tantric union with Mandarava. A Buddhist pilgrim would plan to be at Tso Pema, as it is now known, or Lotus Lake, on this particular day, as the alignment of energies would favor great blessing. Padmasambhava promised to be present to anyone who called on him with devotion on the tenth day of the month, especially in the first lunar month of the year.

The twenty-fifth day is sacred to the dakini, the embodiment of female wisdom. Dakinis are often depicted as guides in Tibetan Tantric Buddhism, and they can take any form: human, celestial, animal, or spirit. They may be beautiful or hideous, fierce or peaceful. Playful, provocative, and prophetic, their function is to awaken authentic being. They act as psychic detonators, stripping away layers of conditioning. Dakini energy is the cutting edge of wisdom. In human form, dakinis are highly evolved women, often the consorts of great yogis. Tantric literature abounds with exotic descriptions of dakinis, from the wild, one-eyed, one-toothed Ekajati to the graceful, nurturing Green Tara. Invoking some form of the dakini on this day can bring blessing to a new project.

In Tibet, where the elemental forces were particularly wild, there were powerful entities controlling mountains, lakes, or rivers. There were also numerous fierce protectors belonging to the indigenous pre-Buddhist shamanistic religion of Tibet, the Bon. Although a significant proportion of these elemental spirits and protectors were subjugated and bound under oath to Buddhism during the eighth century, three hundred years later the yogi Milarepa still encountered the hostile energies of local spirits or demons when he meditated in mountain caves. So the twenty-ninth day is special to the enlightened-wisdom Protectors who guard those on the Buddhist path from harmful spirits, accidents, untimely death, illness, and all manner of obstacles. These deities are immensely wrathful, sometimes sporting snakes as ornaments, brandishing dagger-shaped objects, wearing leopard skins, and standing on corpses, encircled in flames. From electrifying topknot to taut upturned toe, they express the cosmic rage of wrathful compassion.

There are four other specially significant days: the day of miracles in the spring when the Buddha demonstrated his enlightened powers; the late spring or early summer full moon day of his enlightenment and subsequent parinirvana; the summer day seven weeks later when he first taught the dharma, or path, leading to enlightenment; and the autumn day celebrating his descent from the god realms, where he taught his mother and other pure beings. On these days it is said the effect of both good and bad deeds is multiplied 100,000 times. The entire first month of the new year is one in which deeds multiply 100,000 times, as is the special month of the Buddha's birth, enlightenment, and parinirvana.

Although the special days are particular to Tibetan Tantric Buddhism, the quotations are drawn from all Buddhist traditions, from Theravadin to Zen. How did these different traditions evolve? There is no Buddhist "bible," words engraved in stone to last as eternal reference points. In fact, the first discourses of the Buddha were an oral tradition,

A Kingfisher and a Lotus
KOSON, 1877–1945

written down only about four hundred years after his passing. Quite simply, the Buddha taught in accordance with the varying levels and karmic tendencies of different beings. In the first turning of the wheel of dharma at the Deer Park in Sarnath, he laid the foundations of the path: waking up to suffering, renouncing worldly pleasures, observing moral conduct, practicing mindfulness meditation, and understanding the psychology of sensory relating. These teachings form the basis of the Hinayana, or lesser vehicle, emphasized by Theravadin Buddhists in Sri Lanka, Burma, and Thailand. Theravadin wisdom is earth-bound, supremely rational, and healthily restrictive.

In the second turning of the wheel of dharma on a mountain known as Vulture's Peak, the Buddha taught transcendent wisdom or emptiness to highly advanced disciples and celestial beings. And in the third turning at a place of supernatural beings, he refined the teachings on emptiness or Absolute Truth, performing many miracles to demonstrate his point. The second and third cycles of teaching contain the full meaning of the Mahayana, or greater vehicle. As the name suggests, this is a more open, broader path. It's not that the restrictions of the Hinayana have been abandoned, but the viewpoint of transcendent wisdom is vast. A person who is established on the Mahayana path is called a bodhisattva, one who is awakened to the truth. What is awakened is the boundless heart of compassion. Mahayana wisdom is expansive, all-encompassing, and nurturing.

Both Tantric Buddhism, which developed most strongly in Tibet and the northern Himalayan countries of Bhutan, Sikkim, and Nepal, and Zen Buddhism, which developed in Japan and China – where it was called Ch'an – are aspects of the Mahayana. Accounts of Tantric teachings indicate that Tantra was originally revelation. The Buddha transformed himself into the deity at the center of the mandala and bestowed empowerments upon highly developed disciples, enabling them to transform impure phenomenal appearances into wisdom. So Tantra is a sublime path, emphasizing transformation. Tantric wisdom is exalted, exotic, esoteric, ecstatic.

Zen or Ch'an, on the other hand, is a straight pointing to the highest truth, a direct mind-to-mind transmission. It originated with a wordless communication of the Buddha that enabled his disciple, Mahakashyapa, to apprehend ultimate reality directly. Zen wisdom is poetic, imagistic, simple, profound, and nonintellectual.

Norma Levine

NORMA LEVINE

AWAKENING

SPRING

MARCH ✤ APRIL ✤ MAY

Awakening in the Buddhist path means waking up to the suffering inherent in the human condition: the impermanence of conditioned phenomena and the cyclic nature of worldly existence rooted in ignorance, craving, and aversion; culminating in old age, sickness, and death. Understanding the preciousness of the human body to carry one to the shore beyond suffering is the bud of spiritual development, a natural occurrence.

Whether the awakening is gradual or sudden, it is enhanced by moral conduct and mindfulness meditation. The goal of Buddhism is to realize that mind is Buddha. Awakening the Buddha within, one becomes perfect.

The good news is that the seed of the awakened mind doesn't have to be sown. It's already there. Buddhists call it Buddha-nature because it's inherent in every living being. The Indian sage Nagarjuna wrote this in the second century:

When it is springtime,
People say water is warm.
In wintertime,
They say it is cold.
Likewise, when Buddha-nature is completely covered by
*   the nest of passions,*
It is called sentient beings.
When Buddha-nature is separated from the passions,
It is called Buddha.

THINLEY NORBU
White Sail

We need only to be confident we have it, to get in touch with it more and more, and let it be. The eleventh-century Indian mahasiddha, Tilopa – whose name means "sesame seed master" – became enlightened while extracting oil from sesame seeds.

Sesame oil is the essence.
Although the ignorant know that it is in the sesame seed,
They do not understand the way of cause, effect, and
*   becoming,*
And therefore are not able to extract the essence,
*   the sesame oil.*
Although innate coemergent wisdom
Abides in the heart of all beings,
If it is not shown by the guru, it cannot be realized.
Just like the sesame oil that remains in the seed, it does
*   not appear.*
One removes the husk by beating the sesame,
And the sesame oil, the essence appears.
In the same way the guru shows the truth of tathata
*   [the way it is]*
And all phenomena become indivisible in one essence.

CHOGYAM TRUNGPA
AND NALANDA TRANSLATION COMMITTEE
Rain of Wisdom

In the Buddhist view there are three kinds of dreams: the dream of nighttime, which ends at daybreak; the dream of each lifetime, which ends at death; and the dream of ignorance, which ends with enlightenment. Ignorance is thus the root cause of all kinds of dreaming, producing patterns of defiled emotion – pride, anger, jealousy, passion – that create turbulent mind-waves. There is no beginning to the world of ignorance, or samsara, because it arises instantly, moment by moment, as we grasp and cling to things. It ends only when we take back our projections and wake fully to our inherent nature. Buddha-nature lies buried within, like water underground, the uncontaminated source of our authentic being.

So spring is a time for going back to the beginning, looking at the projector rather than the projection. It's a time to acknowledge the suffering that is inherent in ignorance. It's a time to wake up from the drugged sleep of samsara with its consistent cycle of old age, sickness, and death, a time to shine the sun of awareness on the healthy seeds of our inherent nature and allow them to grow.

The day after the new moon in February or early March marks the first day of the Tibetan/Chinese New Year. The first two weeks celebrate one of four major events in the Buddhist calendar: the fifteen days in which, to increase the devotion of future disciples, the Buddha displayed a series of miracles, such as emanating different enlightened forms of himself. The Full Moon Day marks the culmination of this cycle of miracles. According to the Tibetan tradition, during the month of "monlam," the effects of deeds multiply 100,000 times.

The birth, enlightenment, and parinirvana of the Buddha is celebrated in late spring or early summer in the Tibetan tradition, while the Zen tradition places it in the winter. Wesak, which is the festival of the triple event of the Buddha's birth, enlightenment, and parinirvana in the Theravadin tradition, falls on the full moon in May. In honor of this popular tradition, the Buddha's birth, enlightenment, and parinirvana is placed in the spring section.

Crescent Moon over Clouds at Dawn
KAZ MORI

MEDICINE BUDDHA DAY

EIGHTH DAY OF THE MONTH

**THOU ART THE KING PHYSICIAN
WHO DESTROYS OLD AGE, ILLNESS AND DEATH.**

CHARLES LUK (*trans.*)
Vimalakirti Nirdesa Sutra

In many of the Buddhist teachings, illness is considered to have roots in negative emotions. A mind poisoned with passion and aggression, based on deluded perceptions of how things actually are, is a diseased mind. As this is the way of the world, or samsara, and we're in it till we wake up completely, we're all more or less seriously ill even when we think we're healthy. The Buddha is often described as the king of physicians and the dharma as the medicine.

*I am the one whose presence in the world
Is very rarely come upon,
I am the Fully Enlightened One,
I ... am the supreme physician.*

THE BUDDHA, BHIKKU NANAMOLI (*trans.*)
Sela Sutra, *The Middle Length Discourses
of the Buddha*

Countless kinds of purity and cleanness produce the body of the Tathagata. Virtuous ones, if you want to realize the Buddha body in order to get rid of all the illnesses of a living being, you should set yourself on the quest of supreme enlightenment.

THE BUDDHA, CHARLES LUK (*trans.*)
Vimalakirti Nirdesa Sutra

❋ THE PRECIOUSNESS of dharma as medicine is one of the great themes of Mahayana Buddhism. In this brief excerpt from Shantideva's classic text of 187 stanzas on the awakening heart, he states it very clearly:

If I need to comply with a doctor's advice
When frightened by a common illness,
Then how much more so when perpetually diseased
By the manifold evils of desire...

And if all people dwelling on this earth
Can be overcome by just one of these,
And if no other medicine to cure them
Is to be found elsewhere in the universe,

Then the intention not to act in accordance
With the advice of the all-knowing Physicians
Who can uproot every misery,
Is extremely bewildered and worthy of scorn.

SHANTIDEVA, STEPHEN BATCHELOR (*trans.*)
A Guide to the Bodhisattva's Way of Life

❋ THIS TIBETAN teaching offers the classic Buddhist view of the ills of the world.

Seeing that this chronic disease of cherishing myself
Is the cause that gives rise to unwanted suffering,
I seek your blessings to destroy this great demon
   of selfishness
By resenting it as the object of blame.

PANCHEN LOSANG CHOKYI GYALTSAN,
GESHE KELSANG GYATSO (*trans.*)
Offering to the Spiritual Guide

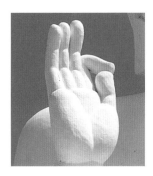

PADMASAMBHAVA DAY

**THE EXPERIENCE THAT HAS TAKEN PLACE IN OUR LIFE SITUATION
IS LIKE THE MUD SURROUNDING THE ROOTS OF THE LOTUS...
THERE IS DESIRE, PASSION, AGGRESSION, NEUROSIS OF ALL KINDS.**

CHOGYAM TRUNGPA
Crazy Wisdom

ॐ

Padmasambhava, affectionately called Guru Rinpoche – Precious Teacher – by Tibetans, is the Tantric Buddha of Tibet. He displayed different forms, among them eight special ones to tame beings according to their circumstances. In the spring, he renounced his kingdom, practiced yoga in the great charnel ground of Sitavana in India, attained liberation, and became known as the Guardian of Peace. He also took monastic ordination from the Buddha's disciple Ananda, mastered all the teachings, and became known as the Lion of the Shakyas. When the king of Zahor in India tried to burn him alive, he transformed the fire into a lake and took the king's daughter, Mandarava, as his consort. He then became known as the Immortal Lotus Born Guru.

This prayer by the Seventh Dalai Lama is part of the great treasury of Tibetan hymns devoted to the heroic activity of the Tantric Buddha.

*Detail of Tibetan figure
of Padmasambhava*

A PRAYER TO THE LOTUS BORN

In the northwestern land
  of Urgyen,
a magically produced valley
  of perfection,
  there springs forth
  a mighty lotus blossom
and upon it appears a wondrous
  and magical transformation.

There sits the Lotus Born Guru,
  a holder of
  diamond knowledge,
who wields in his hand a radiant
  vajra blazing
with the fearless power of wisdom
  gazing boldly at truth.

O Lotus Born One and your
  eight emanations
who inspire strength able to overcome
  every hindrance:
  pacify the conditions
  that bring harm to living beings
  and unfold every circumstance
  conducive to goodness, light
  and liberation.

THE SEVENTH DALAI LAMA,
GLENN H. MULLIN (*trans.*)
Selected Works of the Dalai Lama VII:
Songs of Spiritual Change

ON A very down-to-earth level, Thich Nhat Hanh reminds us that negative emotions such as anger can be transformed by practicing simple awareness. Transformation of the emotions is accomplished by fearlessly penetrating their essence.

When we are angry, we are the anger. When anger is born in us, we can be aware that anger is an energy in us, and we can accept that energy in order to transform it into another kind of energy. When we have a compost bin filled with organic material which is decomposing and smelly, we know that we can transform the waste into beautiful flowers. At first, we may see the compost and the flowers as opposite, but when we look deeply, we see that the flowers already exist in the compost, and the compost already exists in the flowers … It takes only a few months for compost to give birth to flowers. We need the insight and nondual vision of the organic gardener with regard to our anger. We need not be afraid of it or reject it. We know that anger can be a kind of compost, and that it is within its power to give birth to something beautiful. We need anger in the way the organic gardener needs compost … Gradually we can transform our anger completely into peace, love, and understanding.

THICH NHAT HANH
Peace Is Every Step

FULL MOON DAY

FIFTEENTH DAY OF THE MONTH

NOBLY BORN ONES! THE NATURAL STATE OF MIND IS INTRINSICALLY LUMINOUS, INTRINSICALLY DEVOID OF INHERENT EXISTENCE.

THE BUDDHA
Nirvana Sutra, *Tibetan Tripataka*

The example of the full moon is frequently used to point out the nature of mind. It illuminates the darkness, it is cool, clear, tranquil, and its reflection in water is perfect. Similarly, the natural state of mind is intrinsically luminous, and like the reflection of the moon in water, it appears when the surface is calm.

Buddhist wisdom on the spring full moon tells us to light the lamp of awareness so that it illuminates the entire world. It is, in fact, the source of peace itself.

Zen poetry uses the full moon to create imagery that bypasses the intellect.

Reflections of Moon in the Water

WE DON'T have to go looking in far-off, exotic places for Buddha-nature. It's the intrinsic state of our mind. Be still, listen, look, and feel.

The moon of the bodhisattva,
Clear and cool,
Floats in the empty sky.
If the mind of a sentient being
Tranquilizes itself
And becomes like a calm lake,
The beautiful image of bodhi
Will appear there in no time.

LOUIS NORDSTROM
(*trans.*)
Namu Dai Bosa

Didn't I tell you it was there?
You could have found it without trouble, after all.
The south wind is warm;
The sun shines peacefully;
The birds warble their glad songs.
Spring blossoms in the treetops.

LOUIS NORDSTROM (*trans.*)
Namu Dai Bosa

❋ BUDDHISM IS thought to emphasize introspection at the expense of social engagement. But illuminating the inner darkness is the true revolution.

To try to make the whole world truthful would be like trying to cover the whole world with soft leather. Imagine how much soft leather we would need, but how easy it would then be to walk around the whole world. That is impossible, of course. However...if we wear a pair of soft leather shoes, then it is the same as if the whole world were covered with soft leather.

To make a roof which covers the whole world would be impossible. If we had a roof we would never get wet even if it rained...

In this way, for the world to become totally peaceful at one time, to try and make the whole world peaceful as the ideal in one's life, is impossible...

However, if from within our own deep mind, that mind of no disturbance and delusion, that mind with clarity and freedom, we are awakened..., then all of society becomes that ideal society. If within each of us that ideal mind is realized, the Buddha-nature from within each of us...[it] is the same as this whole world becoming peaceful. It is the source of the peace of the whole world.

All of us must first realize our Buddha-nature, give great illumination to that Buddha-nature and with it bring light to all of society. If every single person...receives this Buddha-nature, then that brilliance will fill all of society ... to every single corner.

EKAI KAWAGUCHI ROSHI, SHODA HARADA *(comp.)*
Morning Dewdrops of the Mind

❋ AWARENESS IS born from mindfulness. Lighting the lamp of awareness is like waking up with the full moon shining in the room.

In his novel The Stranger, *Albert Camus describes his antihero as a man who "lives as though dead." This is like living in a dark room with no light of awareness. When you light the lamp of awareness, you pass from sleep to awakening. The verb* buddh *in Sanskrit means "to wake up," and one who wakes up is called a Buddha. A Buddha is a person who is always awake. From time to time we have this awareness, so we are "from-time-to-time" Buddhas.*

THICH NHAT HANH
The Sun My Heart

❋ IN THE first turning of the wheel of dharma, the Buddha emphasized mindfulness of every aspect of the body.

He who has perfected, well developed and practiced in due order mindfulness of breathing, as taught by the Buddha, illuminates this world like the moon released from a cloud.

K. R. NORMAN *(trans.)*
The Elder's Verses: Theragatha and Therigatha,
verses 548–9

DAKINI DAY
TWENTY-FIFTH DAY OF THE MONTH

ONE MUST NOT DISPARAGE WOMEN
ONE SHOULD SPEAK WITH PLEASANT WORDS
AND GIVE A WOMAN WHAT SHE WANTS.

MIRANDA SHAW
Candamaharosana Tantra, *Passionate Enlightenment*

of wisdom, or dakinis, embracing their partners, the five wisdom Buddhas.

The deity Tara is adored by Tibetans as a celestial dakini, the embodiment of compassion. She is a potent archetype who appears in both peaceful and wrathful forms, a saviouress whose powers are vast.

I bow to the Body of Tara, supporting like Earth.
I bow to the Body of Tara, cohering like water.
I bow to the Body of Tara, ripening like fire.
I bow to the Body of Tara, expanding like air.

I bow to the Body of Tara who is the Sovereign of Doctors.
I bow to the Body of Tara subduing disease like medicine.
I bow to the Body of Tara, the river of compassion.
I bow to the Body of Tara skilled in means of taming.
I bow to the Body of Tara lovely but free of desire.
I bow to the Body of Tara who teaches the way to Freedom.

MATRCETA, MARTIN WILSON (*trans.*)
In Praise of Tara

The elements are at their most vibrant in the spring. Our environment energizes us, balancing and restoring vitality. In Tantric Buddhism the purified forms of the five elements – earth, fire, air, water, and space – are depicted as female embodiments

❀ THIS "Song of the Dakini" shows the many faces
of the primordial wisdom goddess.

I praise the Queen of Means who goes gathering riches,
The Queen of Wisdom who subdues the three-fold world,
The dancer in the womb of all-pervading goodness,
I praise the one who overcomes and calms.

Peacemaker, who sends out the light of quietness,
Whose beaming smile lies behind the world,
Who gathers up the ocean of life's bounty
Into the womb of gladness, you I praise.

. . . Passionate, ruddy-faced, you calmly dance;
You are the great enchantress of true love.
O let me praise you as the dakini
Whose passions are unfettered, unperturbed.

Wrathful and cruel with red eyes glaring
You shatter the rigid barriers of the dark.
O let me praise you whose miraculous anger
Is for the sufferer the way to joy.

. . . The cruel devils and the harmless gods
And the gray folk that hustle in between

Make up the array of these impulses.
Command the onslaught and commence attack!

Keep the path clear of those too youthful
And, whether as human being or as goddess,
Devil or vampire, dance entrancingly;
For each of us disperse the darkness of this age.

Among the Buddhas you are a Vajra-yogini,
In the land of Karma you are a great hostess,
On earth you bear a hundred thousand names,
Formless, you yet sum up the universe.

As mother of us, or as daughter,
Take us to where we realize the truth.

In the sea of my mind the words as waves have risen
In recollection of the Great Queen.
May the Ocean benefit
Those who sail beyond the great sea.

CHOGYAM TRUNGPA
Mudra

PROTECTOR DAY
TWENTY-NINTH DAY OF THE MONTH
PROTECTING ONESELF ONE PROTECTS OTHERS;
PROTECTING OTHERS ONE PROTECTS ONESELF.

L. FREER (*ed.*)
Samyutta Nikaya, vol. V

In the Theravadin teachings, the Buddha emphasizes self-reliance. In other words, everything harmful comes from an undisciplined mind. External enemies can harm only if we have not purified our own aggression. When the Buddha's malevolent cousin Devadatta tried to kill him by sending a crazed elephant in his path, the Buddha enveloped the beast with loving-kindness. So powerful was this energy that the elephant stopped in his tracks and bowed his trunk before the Master.

So, the message of Protector Day in the spring is to subdue one's passions fearlessly. The universe will respond.

If you would fight an enemy who harms you,
Then subdue your own passions.
Thus you shall be perfectly free from harm;
For it is on account of your passions that
From the beginning you have been wandering
in the world.

NAGARJUNA AND SAKYA PANDITA
Elegant Sayings

✲ ONE OF the most dramatic statements of awakening to the unending cycle of existence and seeking protection from it was expressed by Naropa. He was a great scholar at Nalanda University in eleventh-century India. Academically, he was unrivaled. But one day, he realized the futility of this kind of knowledge to protect him from the ocean of suffering.

Samsara is the tendency to find fault with others,
An unbearable fire-bowl,
A dungeon dark,
A deep swamp of three poisons,
A fearful wave of evil lives,
'Tis being caught in a spider's web,
Or a bird entangled in a fowler's net,
… It is a fragile water-plant,
The intangible reflection of the moon in water,
A bubble of bewilderment,
Fleeting mist and rippling water,
… A taste of honey on a razor blade,
It is a tree with poisonous leaves,
Shooting the poisoned arrow of disturbed emotions,
… It is a flame flickering in the wind,
Untruth, a dream, bewilderment,
The waterfall of old age and death,
… Verily, I must seek out the Guru.

NAROPA, HERBERT GUENTHER (*trans.*)
The Life and Teaching of Naropa

NEW MOON DAY

THIRTIETH DAY OF THE MONTH

SHOULD THE BUDDHA NOT HAVE BEEN BORN;
HAD THE DHARMA NOT COME OVER FROM INDIA,
BUDDHA'S LAWS WOULD STILL OMNIPRESENTLY HOLD.
SEE HOW THE FLOWERS OPEN IN THE SPRING WIND.

JAIHIUN KIM
Poems by Zen Masters

The new moon in spring is fresh with the promise of hope. It represents growth, the beginning of a new cycle. Buddhist wisdom tells us it's a chance to break out of the cycle altogether, to abandon cherished ideals such as hope, and to start living nakedly, without clinging to the future. Then spiritual growth becomes a natural unfolding, like flowers opening in the wind.

The day after the new moon in either February or March is the first day of the Tibetan New Year, a time of prayers and festivity. On this day, Tibetans wake at dawn, put on new clothes, and throng to the prayer halls of monasteries to offer white greeting scarves and receive a blessing from the resident lama. In fact, the Buddhist perspective of time is nonchronological. Any new year is only a conventional demarcation in what actually has no beginning or end. Instead, the Buddha taught a continuously repeating twelve-linked chain of interdependence starting with ignorance and culminating in old age and death.

Becoming's Wheel reveals no known beginning,
No maker, no experiencer there.
Void with a twelvefold voidness,
Nowhere does it ever halt,
Forever does it spin.

TARTHANG TULKU
Bhanantacariya Buddhaghosa, *Crystal Mirror*

SO HOW do we begin to cut through the spinning wheel? The teachings of contemporary Tibetan Buddhist master Chogyam Trungpa have an unmistakable flavor: direct, pungent, clear, and often provocative. He reminds us that the beginning is NOW.

In meditation we work on ... the projector rather than the projection. We turn inward, instead of trying to sort out external problems ... We work on the creator of duality rather than the creation. That is beginning at the beginning.

CHOGYAM TRUNGPA
The Heart of the Buddha

✤ THE POINT is to be fresh, like spring itself, unburdened with expectations. This quotation from the great Zen master Shunryu Suzuki has become somewhat famous.

In the beginner's mind there are many possibilities, but in the expert's there are few...

We must have beginner's mind, free from possessing anything, a mind that knows everything is in flowing change. Nothing exists but momentarily in its present form and color. One thing flows into another and cannot be grasped. Before the rain stops we hear a bird. Even under the heavy snow we see snowdrops and some new growth.

SHUNRYU SUZUKI
Zen Mind, Beginner's Mind

✤ ACHAAN CHAH, a contemporary Thai master in the Theravadin tradition, teaches as he lived, with natural simplicity and down-to-earth common sense.

The Buddha taught that with things that come about on their own, once you have done the work you can leave the results to nature, to the power of your accumulated karma. Yet your ... effort should not cease. Whether the fruit of wisdom comes quickly or slowly, you cannot force it, just as you cannot force the growth of a tree you have planted. The tree has its own pace. Your job is to dig a hole, water, and fertilize it, and protect it from insects ... the way the tree grows is up to the tree ...

Thus, you must understand the difference between your work and the plant's work. Leave the plant's business to the plant, and be responsible for your own. If the mind does not know what it needs to do, it will try to force the plant to grow ... flower and give fruit in one day. This is ... a major cause of suffering. Just practice in the right direction and leave the rest to your karma. Then whether it takes one hundred or one thousand lifetimes, your practice will be at peace.

ACHAAN CHAH
J. KORNFIELD AND PAUL BREITER *(comp. and ed.)*
A Still Forest Pool

✤ CONTEMPORARY VIETNAMESE Zen master Thich Nhat Hanh is an influential teacher of Buddhism today. Here he emphasizes cultivating healthy seeds.

There are many kinds of seeds in us, both good and bad ... In a tiny grain of corn there is the knowledge, transmitted by previous generations, of how to sprout and how to make leaves, flowers, and ears of corn ... Our ancestors ... have given us seeds of joy, peace, and happiness, as well as seeds of sorrow, anger ...

Every time we practice mindful living, we plant healthy seeds and strengthen the healthy seeds already in us. Healthy seeds function similarly to antibodies ... If we plant wholesome, healing, refreshing seeds, they will take care of the negative seeds ... To succeed we need to cultivate a good reserve of refreshing seeds.

THICH NHAT HANH
Peace Is Every Step

CELEBRATION OF MIRACLES

FESTIVAL DAY ~ FIFTEENTH DAY OF THE FIRST LUNAR MONTH

WHILE DELUDED, ONE IS USED BY THIS BODY;

WHEN ENLIGHTENED, ONE USES THIS BODY.

TAISEN DESHIMARU
Sayings of Bunan, *The Ring of the Way*

༄

The first two weeks of the new year in the spring culminate in the Full Moon Day, which commemorates the Buddha's display of miracles and marks the first of four extraordinary days in the Buddhist year. The occasion is well documented in the life of the Buddha. At a place called Shravasti he encountered the hostility of six heretical masters, one of them being Mahavira, the founder of the Jains. The others were materialists, determinists, or skeptics. The Buddha triumphed over all of them and sealed his victory by manifesting miracles: jets of water and rays of light, the miraculous growth of an enormous mango tree, the multiplication of imaginary Buddhas, walking in the sky, after which he went to the god realm and returned with Brahma and Indra on three precious ladders.

How do miraculous powers happen? It's somehow refreshing to hear that in the first turning of the wheel of dharma, the Buddha attributes miraculous powers to the strict observation of the basic precepts of moral conduct and right living in any human culture: not killing, not lying, not stealing, abstaining from sexual misconduct and intoxicants. Without this foundation, there are no miracles.

If a bhikku should wish: "May I wield the various kinds of supernormal power: having been one, may I become many; having been many, may I become one; may I appear and vanish; may I go unhindered through a wall, through an enclosure, through a mountain as though through space; may I dive in and out of the earth as though it were water; may I walk on water without sinking as though it were earth; seated crosslegged, may I travel in space like a bird; with my hand may I touch and stroke the moon and sun so powerful and mighty; may I wield bodily mastery, even as far as the Brahma-world," let him fulfill the precepts ...

BHIKKU NANAMOLI (*trans.*)
Akankheyya Sutra, verse 14,
The Middle Length Discourses of the Buddha

✳ THE TIBETAN celebration of the Buddha's display of miracles is called Monlam Chenmo – great auspiciousness. The manner of celebrating it originated in 1409 with the great monk and teacher Je Tsongkhapa. Tens of thousands of monks, watched by an equal number of laypeople, participated in dramatic philosophical debates. There were prayers, songs, ritual dances, and huge offerings of food and drink to the destitute.

The celebration of generosity culminates in a teaching by the Dalai Lama on the Buddha's previous lives, a tradition started by the thirteenth Dalai Lama, whose favorite story was the famous "Tale of the Tigress," in which a young Brahmin hermit is the Buddha in a previous life.

Tigress and Cubs

A young Brahmin of renowned family showed clear intellect early in life, which led him into a forest retreat. He had concluded that desire for the pleasures of this world was the cause of suffering.

Noticeable changes occurred in his environment after his arrival. The wild animals who had lived there for centuries no longer harmed one another ... Many human disciples wandered his way. He taught them the dharma.

One day he walked with a disciple, Ajita, up the mountain. Standing at the top of a cliff, they paused to survey the peaks. But their attention was drawn to what they heard from below – the pitiful sound of hungry young animals. They heard too a fierce growling. Then they realized that they had come upon a tigress and her cubs and that the tigress, starving, was menacing the cubs.

"Go find her food as quickly as possible," the bodhisattva [Brahmin] told Ajita, who immediately began the search. Alone, the bodhisattva entered upon a soliloquy in praise of generosity, giving physical possessions to those in need.

He concluded by hurling himself off the cliff into the den of the tigress below. The fall killed him, flesh and bone hitting hard earth from a great height. The tigress ate him. She didn't eat her cubs.

DALAI LAMA *(commentary)*
Generous Wisdom

BIRTH OF THE BUDDHA

FESTIVAL DAY ~ FULL MOON IN MAY

**AFTER HIS BIRTH THE INFANT BUDDHA WALKED FOUR DIRECTIONS WITH SEVEN PACES.
BRAVELY AND GRACEFULLY EIGHT THOUSAND TIMES IN THE PAST
HE HAS COME INTO THIS WORLD AND HAS GONE FROM IT AGAIN.**

LOUIS NORDSTROM (*ed.*)
Commemoration of Buddha's Birth, 7 April 1946, Los Angeles
Namu Dai Bosa

Naturally, the birth of Prince Siddhartha was wondrous. His mother, Queen Mahamaya, had a dream prior to the birth of a magnificent white elephant that descended from the heavens. Celestial music sounding praises filled the sky. The elephant held a brilliant pink lotus flower in its trunk, placed it within the queen's body, and then entered inside her effortlessly. She awoke filled with sensations of pure bliss and joy. Ten months later, on the way to her parents' home, she stopped to rest in the garden of Lumbini, and there, holding the branch of an ashok tree for support, the queen gave birth to a radiant boy.

When the Bodhisattva came forth from his mother's womb, two jets of water appeared to pour from the sky, one cool and one warm for bathing the Bodhisattva and his mother. As soon as the Bodhisattva was born, he stood firmly with his feet on the ground, then he took seven steps to the north, and with a white sunshade held over him, he surveyed each quarter. He uttered the words, "I am the highest in the world, I am the best in the world, I am the foremost in the world; this is the last birth; now there is no more renewal of being in future lives."

… A great measureless light surpassing the splendor of the gods appeared … And even in those abysmal world interspaces of vacancy, gloom, and utter darkness, where the moon and sun, powerful and mighty as they are, cannot make their light prevail – there too a great measureless light … appeared … And this ten thousand-fold world element shook and quaked and trembled …

*His color was as pure
As beams of brilliant gold wrought in a crucible,
Shining and clear.
… Dazzling as the cloudless autumn sky;
While gods in the heavenly vault held over him
A many-ribbed sunshade with a thousand circles,
Brandishing gold-sticked chowries …*

BHIKKU NANAMOLI (*trans.*)
The Life of the Buddha

❋ IT IS said that the lives of every Buddha, past and future; show twelve deeds: remaining in Tushita heaven; descent and entry into the womb; taking birth; proficiency in the arts; enjoyment of consorts; renouncing the world; practicing asceticism; reaching the point of enlightenment; vanquishing temptations; attaining perfect enlightenment; turning the doctrinal wheel; and passing into nirvana.

This excerpt from a poem entitled "The Twelve Deeds of Lord Buddha," by contemporary Tibetan master Tai Situpa, describes three of the twelve deeds.

Because you could hear the saddening cries of suffering
And the calling of your children from a ripening world,
To fulfill the hopes and wishes of those beings,
To bring them to happiness and show virtue's worth,
With limitless love and fearless resolution
From the highest of Pure Lands you emanated to earth.
Great is the Buddha.

Seeing Jambudvipa, our planet, in extraordinary
*   vision,*
A mother who could bear you, a father a great king,
With courage that was born of the deepest conviction
In the benefit that your life as a human would bring,
Amidst miracles and wonders, you entered the womb
Of noble Mahamaya, King Suddhodhana's queen.
Great is the Buddha.

Born painlessly from her right side in the grove
*   of Lumbini,*
With the special signs of a Buddha your body
*   was marked;*
You took seven steps in each of the principal directions
And at each step a lotus flower sprang up from the earth.
The Lord of Gods came to make his humble prostration
As you declared yourself most high in the whole universe.
Great is the Buddha.

TAI SITUPA
The Twelve Deeds of Lord Buddha

❋ WITH MINDFULNESS, the activity is unimportant. Even washing dishes is as sacred as bathing a Buddha.

Each bowl I wash, each poem I compose … is a miracle, and each has exactly the same value. One day while washing a bowl, I felt that my movements were as sacred as bathing a newborn Buddha. If he were to read this, that newborn Buddha would certainly be happy for me, and not at all insulted …

Each thought, each action in the sunlight of awareness becomes sacred. In this light no boundary exists between the sacred and the profane.

THICH NHAT HANH
The Sun My Heart

ENLIGHTENMENT

FESTIVAL DAY ~ FULL MOON IN MAY

**WHAT IS ENLIGHTENMENT? IT IS TO KNOW YOUR MIND AS IT REALLY IS...
ENLIGHTENMENT HAS THE SAME ATTRIBUTE AS SPACE. THEREIN THERE IS NEITHER
THAT WHICH BECOMES ENLIGHTENED NOR THAT TO WHICH ONE IS ENLIGHTENED.**

Maha-vairochana Tantra,
Taisho Shinshu Daizokyo Kyokai

After years of practicing unimaginable austerities so that "all my limbs became like the knotted joints of withered creepers" and "the skin of my belly and back met," the monk Gautama – as Prince Siddhartha was then called – was near extinction but no closer to enlightenment. A young village girl, Sujata, lovingly prepared a bowl of fresh milk with rice and graciously offered it to the emaciated ascetic. His senses immediately became alert.

Sitting under the massive branches of a bodhi tree, in what is now Bodh Gaya, Gautama began the world-shattering seven-day meditative insight that resulted in complete enlightenment. Here are first words he spoke as the Buddha.

Seeking but not finding the house-builder,
I traveled through the round of countless births;
O painful is birth ever and again.
House-builder, you have now been seen;
You shall not build the house again.
Your rafters have been broken down;
Your ridge pole is demolished too.
My mind has now attained the unformed nirvana
And reached the end of every kind of craving.

BHIKKU NANAMOLI *(trans.)*
The Life of the Buddha

There was a terrifying thunderstorm in the second watch of the night. When the third watch of the night had passed, the Buddha looked up and saw the morning star dazzling bright as a diamond in the dawn sky. To seal his enlightenment he touched his hand to the ground and said, "The earth is my witness."

When Zen master Seung Sahn visited the bodhi tree in India, he composed this poem.

Once a great man sat beneath the Bodhi tree.
He saw the Eastern star, became enlightened.
He absolutely believed his eyes,
And he believed his ears, his nose, tongue, body,
  and mind.
The sky is blue, the earth is brown,
And so he was awakened to the truth
And attained freedom beyond birth and death.

SEUNG SAHN, IN JACK KORNFIELD
A Path with Heart

BECAUSE NIRVANA is inconceivable, it's often described negatively in the Theravadin tradition as a state of no-thing-ness.

There is an island, an island which you cannot go beyond. It is a place of nothingness, a place of nonpossession and of nonattachment. It is the total end of death and decay, and this is why I call it nirvana (the extinguished, the cool).

SADDHATISSA (*trans.*)
Sutta Nipata, verses 1094–5

SOME TIME after his enlightenment, the Buddha set out on the road to Benares. He passed a monk walking the same road, who remarked on the radiance of his complexion and the serenity of his countenance. "Who is your teacher?" he asked the Buddha.

I have no teacher, and one like me
  Exists nowhere in all the world
  With all its gods, because I have
  No person for my counterpart.

I am the Accomplished One in the world,
  I am the Teacher Supreme.
  I alone am the Fully Enlightened One
  Whose fires are quenched and extinguished.

THE BUDDHA, BHIKKU NANAMOLI (*trans.*)
The Middle Length Discourses of the Buddha

PARINIRVANA

FESTIVAL DAY ~ FULL MOON IN MAY

KNOWING THE BODY IS LIKE FOAM, REALIZING ITS MIRAGE-LIKE NATURE,

CUTTING OFF THE FLOWER-TIPPED SENSUAL REALM,

ONE GOES UNSEEN BY THE KING OF DEATH.

The Dhammapada

૪

The Buddha's death is called parinirvana – passing into nirvana – because there is no death for the enlightened. The container dissolves and the great expanse of space merges with itself. Parinirvana is celebrated as part of the second extraordinary day.

> *He whose passions are destroyed, who is indifferent to food, whose object is the void and the unconditioned freedom, his path cannot be traced like that of birds through the sky.*
>
> *The Dhammapada*

❀ ON THE full moon day in May nearly fifty years after his enlightenment, the Buddha and his disciples walked to the little mud-walled town of Kushinagar near the Nepalese border. He placed himself on his side, facing north, with one foot overlapping the other, mindful and fully aware. Twin sal trees shed blossom out of season to cover him, sandalwood powder fell from the sky, and celestial music resounded. His beloved attendant Ananda wept. "I declare this to you," the Buddha said. "It is in the nature of all formations to dissolve. Attain perfection through diligence."

❀ IN THE *Diamond Sutra*, the Buddha had described the transitory nature of existence – the "baseless fabric of the vision" – in poetry as striking as Shakespeare's *The Tempest*.

> *Thus shall you think of all this fleeting world:*
> *A star at dawn, a bubble in a stream;*
> *A flash of lightning in a summer cloud,*
> *A flickering lamp, a phantom, and a dream.*
>
> A.F. PRICE AND WONG MOU-LAM *(trans.)*
> *The Diamond Sutra*

✻ WHEN THE Buddha announced his imminent death to his grief-stricken disciples, he advised them to shine the light of gnosis on the insubstantial pageant. The Buddha realized what Shakespeare described: "We are such stuff / As dreams are made on, and our little life/ Is rounded with a sleep." Here are the Buddha's last words.

> *Everything comes to an end, though it may last for an aeon … I have done what I could do both for myself and for others … I have disciplined in heaven and on earth, all those whom I could discipline … Hereafter … my dharma … shall abide for generations … among living beings. Therefore, recognize the true nature of the living world and do not be anxious; for separation cannot possibly be avoided …When the light of gnosis has dispelled the darkness of ignorance, when all existence has been seen as without substance, peace ensues [at life's end], which seems to cure a long sickness at last … The time for my entry into nirvana has arrived. These are my last words!*
>
> ASHVAGHOSHA
> *Buddhacarita, vol. xxvi*

✻ THE ELEMENTS of the natural world and the various beings in the different realms of existence responded to the Buddha's passing. Except for some of the gods, who maintained their meditative composure, and Mara's (Temptation's) hosts, who felt they had triumphed and rejoiced, the whole world grieved.

> *When the Sage entered Nirvana, the earth quivered like a ship struck by a squall, and firebrands fell from the sky. The heavens were lit up by a preternatural fire, which burned without fuel, without smoke, without being fanned by the wind. Fearsome thunderbolts crashed down on the earth, and violent winds raged in the sky. The moon's light waned, and in spite of a cloudless sky, an uncanny darkness spread everywhere. The rivers, as if overcome with grief, were filled with boiling water. Beautiful flowers grew out of season on the sal trees above the Buddha's couch, and the trees bent down over him and showered his golden body with their flowers … the five-headed Nagas stood motionless in the sky, their eyes reddened with grief, their hoods closed …with deep devotion they gazed upon the body of the Sage … The Kings of the Gandharvas and Nagas, as well as the Yaksas and the Devas … all stood in the sky … absorbed in the utmost grief … the world, when the Prince of Seers had passed beyond, became like a mountain whose peak has been shattered by a thunderbolt; it became like the sky without the moon, [or] like a pond whose lotuses the frost has withered …*
>
> EDWARD CONZE *(trans.)*
> *Buddhist Scriptures*

ANNIVERSARY OF MILAREPA

FOURTEENTH DAY OF THE FIRST LUNAR MONTH

MILAREPA (1053–1155) IS VENERATED BECAUSE IN ONE LIFETIME HE WENT FROM MURDERER TO BUDDHA, SHOWING THE EFFECTIVENESS OF THE TANTRIC PATH.

The greatest yogi-poet-saint in the history of Tibet, and possibly anywhere, was Milarepa. A legend in his own lifetime, he was a black magician who, if he lived now, would be called a mass murderer. Understanding the suffering he would endure as a result of his evil deeds, he renounced the path of darkness to tread the Buddhist path to enlightenment. In order to purify his karma, he lived in solitude in the mountains and meditated rigorously.

Like a lion, I do not fear;
Like an elephant, I have no anxiety;
Like a madman, I have no pretension and no hope.
I tell you the honest truth.

GARMA C.C. CHANG (*trans.*)
The Hundred Thousand Songs of Milarepa

❊ AS HE wandered through the mountains and villages of Tibet, Milarepa encountered all kinds of people – hunters, old women, farmers. As they exchanged views, Milarepa sang songs of enlightenment to show the way. Meeting a farmer one spring, he sang of plowing and sowing.

In this month of spring the peasants
Of Tibet are busy on their farms.
I, the yogi, also farm.

Upon the bad field of desires,
I spread the fertilizer of the Preparatory Practice;
I wet the field with manure of the Five Nectars;
I plant the seeds of the Nonconfusing Mind,
Farming with discriminative thought.

I plow with Nondualistic oxen,
Harnessed to the Wisdom-Plow,
With Observation of Precepts as the nose-rope,
And Nondistraction effort as the girth.
Diligence is my whip, and skill my bridle.
With these tools and efforts, the bud of Bodhi sprouts;
In due season ripe will be my fruit.

You are a farmer who grows annual crops;
For eternity I cultivate.
At harvest you are proud and joyful.
Which of us will be happier in the end?

GARMA C.C. CHANG (*trans.*)
The Hundred Thousand Songs of Milarepa

ANNIVERSARY OF KUKAI (KOBO DASHAI)

TWENTY-FIRST DAY OF MARCH

**KUKAI (774 –835) IS CONSIDERED THE SPIRITUAL FATHER OF JAPANESE CULTURE.
HE DIED ON 21 MARCH 835.**

Kukai is revered in Japan as the founder of Shingon Buddhism, a form of Japanese Tantra using elaborate rituals to express esoteric truth. He was not only a great saint and visionary – he died in meditation – but also a great writer, poet, calligrapher, scholar, and administrator. He built monasteries and schools, compiled a dictionary, supervised public works projects, and the restoration of Chinese works of art. He was also famous for his occult powers, particularly his ability to make rain. Unsurprisingly, he is considered to be the spiritual father of Japanese culture. Shingon devotees believe he has not died but that he continues to sit in silent meditation. Notwithstanding, after his "death" he was conferred the title of Kobo Dashai, great master of Buddhist teachings.

Kukai's poems express the Buddhist view of the simultaneously occurring emptiness and appearance of phenomena.

SINGING IMAGE OF AN ECHO

In an empty hall of a mouth or canyon
A voice or echo arises from vibrations of the air,
Foolish and wise ones hear it in different ways
As if anger or pleasure are really different.
Seeking the origin, we find that things have no essence.
All is unborn, imperishable, and has no beginning nor end.
Stay in the One Mind of no discrimination.
Voice and echo only deceive the ears.

SINGING IMAGE OF FOAM

A fine rain falls from heaven.
Many kinds of foam spreading on water
Are born then perish without leaving the water.
They are not born from self or other, but from the
chain of causation.
Things arising in visions are mystifying.
Buddhas in the mind make them. Never suspect or
doubt them.
Fundamentally, Truth and Mind are one.
Not to know this is extremely pitiable.

MORGAN GIBSON AND HIROSHI MURAKAMI (*trans.*)
Tantric Poetry of Kukai

37

ANNIVERSARY OF KYONG HO

TWENTY FIFTH DAY OF APRIL

**KYONG HO (1849–1912) DEVOTED HIS LIFE TO
THE REVIVAL OF KOREAN ZEN.**

Zen master Kyong Ho – whose name means Empty Mirror – was a brilliant monk who succeeded in reviving Korean Zen from three hundred years of repression and neglect. By the age of twenty-three, he had mastered the philosophies of Confucianism, Taoism, and Buddhism, and was appointed to the prestigious position of lecturer at the Buddhist College of Tongha-sa. On his way to visit his old master, he passed a mysteriously deserted village. Each door he opened revealed a room full of rotting corpses. The cholera plague had struck! Though he had understood the transient nature of all phenomena, he still felt attached to his body. So he returned to the temple and decided to lock himself in a room until he attained enlightenment. He meditated on a koan for three months. Whenever he felt sleepy, he would take an awl and plunge it into his thigh, or place his jaw on a sharp-edged sword to jolt himself awake.

His big breakthrough came when his devoted attendant told him of a conversation he'd had with a certain Mr. Lee, who said if Kyong Ho continued to meditate by only eating, sitting, and lying down, he would be reborn as a cow without nostrils. When Kyong Ho heard "a cow without nostrils," he broke through his koan and danced cheerfully. A year later he composed a long poem, "Song of Enlightenment."

> *In spring, flowers are in full bloom in the mountain.*
> *In autumn the moon is bright and the wind is cool.*
> *I sing a song of no birth.*
> *But who will ever listen to my song? …*
> *The stone man blows the flute and the wooden man sleeps.*
> *But the common man does not realize his own mind …*
> *Hearing someone say, "a cow without nostrils,"*
> *I realized the true mind,*
> *Where there is no name or form.*
> *I radiate great light in all directions.*
> *The single bright light on the forehead is the Pure Land.*
> *The divine form around the head is God's world.*
> *… Wherever you touch, there is the heavenly truth.*

MU SOENG SUNIM
Thousand Peaks

ANNIVERSARY OF SHINRAN SHONIN

TWENTY–FIRST DAY OF MAY

SHINRAN SHONIN (1173–1262) FOUNDED THE MOST IMPORTANT OF THE PURE LAND SCHOOLS.

In Mahayana Buddhism there is the possibility of enlightenment through unshakable, heartfelt devotion. The red Buddha of the western direction, Amitabha, is said to have manifested a paradise – a Pure Land – and to have vowed to bring to it anyone who called his name with sincere faith.

The Japanese master Shinran is the founder of what is considered to be the most important of the Pure Land schools of Buddhism. It is based on the recitation of Amitabha Buddha's mantra, known as the Nembutsu. Although Amitabha Buddha is acknowledged by all Mahayana Buddhists, single-minded devotion as a doctrine of salvation is fundamental to the Pure Land School. These are Shinran's thoughts on the Nembutsu.

> *Of good and evil I am totally ignorant. If I understood good as Buddha understands it, then I could say I knew what was good. If I understood evil as Buddha understands it, then I could say I knew what was bad. But I am an ordinary mortal, of passion and desire, living in this transient world like the dweller in a house on fire. Every judgment of mine, whatever I say, is nonsense and gibberish. The* Nembutsu *alone is true.*
>
> WILLIAM THEODORE DE BARY *(ed.)*
> *Sources of Japanese Tradition*

BLOSSOMING

SUMMER

JUNE ❁ JULY ❁ AUGUST

The blossoming of Buddhist insight happens with the development of wisdom. The flower of perfection is the Prajnaparamita Sutra, literally transcendent wisdom, in which the Buddha taught the interdependence of all phenomena and their essential emptiness.

The bud of mindfulness and moral conduct results in the flower of wisdom and compassion. The great way opens up, and one who treads on it is called a bodhisattva, or awakened warrior, because his or her heart is open to all of creation. Like the lotus arising from the mud, the bodhisattva is in the world but not overwhelmed by it.

41

After cultivating the seed of awakened mind, experience blossoms, as inevitably as spring buds open into summer flowers. Mind is like a lotus with roots in mud, immaculate flower above the water. Similarly, clarity is the natural expression of mind's expansion from the mud of delusion. In the *Anguttara-nikaya Sutra* the Buddha says:

> As a lotus fair and lovely,
> By the water is not soiled,
> By the world am I not soiled.
> Therefore, Brahmin, am I Buddha.
>
> EDWARD CONZE (*trans. and ed.*)
> *Buddhist Texts through the Ages*

In the world, but above all worldly taints, is the flower of wisdom and compassion, effortlessly benefiting all beings.

> I refresh this entire world
> Like a cloud which releases its rain evenly for all;
> Equal is enlightenment for noble and mean alike
> For those who are immoral and for moral ones.
>
> ... As when it rains the shrubs and grasses,
> The bushes and the smaller plants,
> The trees and also the great woods
> All are made splendid in the ten regions.
>
> So the nature of dharma always exists for the welfare
>   of the world,
> And it refreshes by this dharma the entire world.
> And then refreshed, just like the plants,
> The world will burst forth into blossom.
>
> EDWARD CONZE (*trans. and ed.*)
> *Buddhist Texts through the Ages*

The blossoming of wisdom and compassion is associated with the Mahayana tradition, an expansion that happened about four hundred years after the passing of the Buddha. The occasion was the discovery of certain essential discourses spoken by the Buddha during the second turning of the wheel of dharma. These had been hidden in the water realm of the Nagas under the protection of serpentine guardians of dharma treasure until Buddhist practitioners were mature enough to receive them. The great jewel of dharma discoveries was the *Prajnaparamita Sutra*, a discourse on the true nature of reality.

To set the stage for an event that would break through the veils of illusion, revealing ultimate indescribable reality, the Buddha performed a cosmic miracle.

Thus I once heard. The Lord dwelt on the Vulture Peak at Rajgriha with a large gathering. He sat down cross-legged on his lion throne and entered the "King Samadhi" … His whole body became radiant. The thousand-spoked wheels on the soles of his feet shone forth … light rays, as did every other part of his superhuman body. These light rays illumined …our vast … universe … And all the beings lit up and illuminated by these dazzling light rays became focused upon the unexcelled, true, and perfect enlightenment.

Thereupon … the Lord put out his tongue. With it he covered this entire billion-world universe, and it shone forth … billions of trillions of light rays. Each one of these light rays turned into thousand-petaled golden lotuses, made of the finest jewel substance. On these lotuses were Buddha-emanations giving teachings … And the beings who heard these true teachings became all the more focused on unexcelled, true, perfect enlightenment.

Thereupon the Lord … with his miraculous power … shook this vast billion-world universe in six ways. It became soft and pliable and all beings came to be at

ease. The hells, the underworlds, and the animal realms were abolished and became empty, and all places of horrible rebirth disappeared … beings born blind saw forms, the deaf heard sounds, the insane regained their consciousness, the distracted became concentrated, the hungry were fed, the thirsty were satisfied, the sick were healed, and the cripples were made whole.

LEX HIXON
Mother of the Buddhas

This is a miracle on a cosmic scale, the absolute transformation of the depths of suffering. The expression of transcendent wisdom is limitless compassion. Transcendent wisdom is thus the matrix of all being, the womb of origination. She gives birth to all the buddhas.

The seventh week after the enlightenment marks the third extraordinary day in the Buddhist year: the first turning of the wheel of dharma at the Deer Park in Sarnath. Persuaded by the gods Indra and Brahma to set the wheel of law in motion, the Buddha turned his footsteps toward present-day Varanasi.

*I go to Kasi's city now
To set the wheel of law in motion.
In a blindfold world
I go to beat the deathless drum.*

BHIKKU NANAMOLI
The Life of the Buddha

MEDICINE BUDDHA

EIGHTH DAY OF THE MONTH

COMPASSION FOR ALL CREATURES IS THE TRUE RELIGION.

ASHVAGHOSHA
Buddhacarita

The awakened heart of compassion is the elixir of medicines. This awakened heart is more than pity. It is the spontaneous reflex of wisdom: the deep knowledge of the interdependent web of sentient life and the transitory, ephemeral nature of the bubble we cling to as a self. It's not "I feel sorry for you," but "I am in you, and you in me."

So Medicine Buddha in the summer is very alive, pulsating with the life of the whole universe. Mindfulness has developed into the wisdom that sees everything as it is. And this wisdom is the supreme medicine.

❀ SHANTIDEVA SEEMED lazy and stupid to his fellow monks at the monastic university of Nalanda in eighth-century India; so they asked him to give a discourse. As he delivered a spontaneous poem of 187 stanzas on the awakening heart, he levitated into the sky, stunning the assembly with his supernatural accomplishment. Shantideva's poem on boundless compassion is the heart of the bodhisattva aspiration – to deliver all beings from suffering.

May I be the doctor and the medicine
And may I be the nurse
For all sick beings in the world
Until everyone is healed.

May a rain of food and drink descend
To clear away the pain of thirst and hunger
And during the aeon of famine
May I myself change into food and drink.

... May I be a protector for those without one,
A guide for all travelers on the way;
May I be a bridge, a boat and a ship
For all those who wish to cross (the water).

May I be an island for those who seek one
And a lamp for those desiring light,
May I be a bed for all who wish to rest
And a slave for those who want a slave.

May I be a wishing jewel, a magic vase,
Powerful mantras and great medicine,
May I become a wish-fulfilling tree
And a cow of plenty for the world.

Just like space
And the great elements such as earth,
May I always support the life
Of all the boundless creatures.

And until they pass away from pain
May I also be the source of life
For all the realms of varied beings
That reach unto the ends of space.

Just like a blindman
Discovering a jewel in a heap of rubbish,
Likewise by some coincidence
An Awakening Mind has been born within me.

It is the supreme ambrosia
That overcomes the sovereignty of death.
It is the inexhaustible treasure
That eliminates all poverty in the world.

It is the supreme medicine
That quells the world's disease.

It is the tree that shelters all beings
Wandering and tired on the path of conditioned existence.

It is the universal bridge
That leads to freedom from unhappy states of birth,
It is the dawning moon of the mind
That dispels the torment of disturbing conceptions.

It is the great sun that finally removes
The misty ignorance of the world.
It is the quintessential butter
From the churning of the milk of dharma.

SHANTIDEVA, STEPHEN BATCHELOR (*trans.*)
A Guide to the Bodhisattva's Way of Life

Rain soddens what is covered up.
It does not sodden what is open.
Therefore uncover what is covered,
That the rain will not sodden it.

JOHN D. IRELAND (*trans.*)
The Udana

The virtuous … retain in their mind the good done to them, whereas the evil they experienced drops from their mind like water from a lotus petal.

ERNEST M. BOWDEN (*comp.*)
Jatamakala (story 23, verse 22),
The Imitation of Buddha

PADMASAMBHAVA DAY

TENTH DAY OF THE MONTH

FOR AN INFANT TO BE BORN IN SUCH A WILD, DESOLATE PLACE IN THE MIDDLE OF A LAKE ON A LOTUS IS BEYOND THE GRASP OF CONCEPTUAL MIND ... THAT IS A VERY EXCITING MESSAGE ... ONE CAN BE ENLIGHTENED AND BE INFANT-LIKE ... IF WE ARE AWAKE, WE ARE ONLY AN INFANT ... WE ARE INNOCENT BECAUSE WE HAVE GONE BACK TO OUR ORIGINAL STATE OF BEING.

CHOGYAM TRUNGPA
Crazy Wisdom

An extraordinary event occurred twelve years after the Buddha passed away, something so far-reaching that it shaped Tibetan history and indeed expanded the Buddha's teaching to its full potential. According to the sacred histories, a ray of light went forth from the tongue of Amitabha Buddha (the red Buddha of the western direction), formed into a vajra (the male symbol) and penetrated a lotus (the female symbol) on Dhanakosa Lake, in present-day Pakistan. In due course, a radiant eight-year-old boy was discovered sitting on the lotus. This was the birth of Padmasambhava, the Lotus Born Guru who would manifest the Tantric path – the way to attain enlightenment in one lifetime. Before his parinirvana the Buddha had prophesied:

I will pass away to eradicate the view of permanence.
But twelve years from now, to clear away the view of nihilism,
I shall appear from a lotus in the immaculate Lake Kosha
As a noble son to delight the king
And turn the Dharma wheel of the unexcelled essential meaning

YESHE TSOGYAL, ERIC PEMA KUNSANG (*trans.*)
The Lotus-Born

Tibetan bronze figure of Padmasambhava

KING INDRABHUTI had everything except what he desired the most – a son. When he heard of the eight-year-old boy sitting on the lotus flower of a lake in his kingdom, he went with his minister to see for himself.

ༀ

The king and his minister entered a skiff and arrived at the spot
amid the cries of flocks of scarlet waterbirds.
Sitting on the lotus was a child of beautiful face, a delight to the eyes;
a child one would consider to be eight years old.
The color of his body was like the purple of shells,
and the king marveled:
"Emaho!
Miraculous, admirable child!
Who is your father? Who is your mother?
What is your country? To what caste do you belong?
On what do you nourish yourself? What are you doing here?"
The child replied:
"My father is the Knowing of Knowledge.
My mother is … holy joy and transcendence of the Void.
My country: I have none, having been born on the Essence Plane with its unique caste.
I nourish myself with both clarity and perplexity.
I am here devoting myself to the destruction of suffering."
At these words the king wept profusely
and his blind right eye was … opened …
The prince was named Tsokyi Dorje, Diamond Born of the Lake.

KENNETH DOUGLAS AND GWENDOLYN BAYS (*trans.*)
The Life and Liberation of Padmasambhava

ༀ

The king brought the child back to the palace with him and adopted him as his son and heir.

FULL MOON DAY

THERE IS NO EYE LIKE THAT OF WISDOM.

THERE IS NO NIGHT LIKE SPIRITUAL DARKNESS.

NAGARJUNA AND SAKYA PANDITA
Elegant Sayings

ॐ

The full moon of the Buddha's teaching, the perfect peak of dharma, is the discourse on transcendent wisdom – Prajnaparamita – delivered, appropriately, at Vulture's Peak in India. Transcendent wisdom is the wisdom that goes beyond words and concepts. How can words that form concepts go beyond words and concepts? By continually deconstructing words and concepts. So we learn that this is not a teaching at all, that there is nothing to attain, no one to attain it; and in case we think we have grasped that concept, there is no nonattainer and no nonattainment either. In the absence of all concepts, definitions, limitations, there is blissful, clear, and luminous presence. Transcendent wisdom. Tranquil like the depths of the ocean, and ceaselessly manifesting like waves. Wisdom and compassion. Emptiness and appearance. "Form is emptiness" the sutra says, "but emptiness is also form."

So the full moon in summer is intuitive, ungraspable, feminine. The flower of wisdom and compassion blooms in the sky.

Homage to the Perfection of Wisdom, the lovely, the holy!

… All those who appear as Buddhas in the three times, fully awake to the utmost, right, and perfect enlightenment because they have relied on the perfection of wisdom. Therefore one should know the Prajnaparamita as the great spell, the spell of great knowledge, the utmost spell, the unequaled spell, allayer of all suffering, in truth – for what could go wrong? By the Prajnaparamita has this spell been delivered. It runs like this: Gone, gone, gone beyond, gone altogether beyond, O what an awakening, all hail!

THE BUDDHA,
EDWARD CONZE (*trans.*)
The Perfection of
Wisdom Sutra,
*Buddhist Texts
through the Ages*

❋ BUDDHIST POETRY frequently embodies the experience of transcendent wisdom. No doubt the ultimate truth was also glimpsed by many non-Buddhist poets: Shakespeare, Blake, Yeats, Bob Dylan. But only a fully enlightened one can sustain the vision. As T.S. Eliot said, "Mankind cannot bear too much reality."

We must not regard "knowing" as something from the outside which comes to breathe life into the universe.
It is the dance of the universe itself. The dance and the dancer are one.
Forest.
Thousands of tree-bodies and mine.
Leaves are waving.
Ears hear the streams call.
Eyes see into the sky of mind,
A half-smile unfolds on every leaf.
There is a forest here
Because I am here.
But mind has followed the forest
And clothed itself in green.

THICH NHAT HANH
The Sun My Heart

❋ IN THIS evocative poem, "the sphere of perfect communion," like Prajnaparamita, is feminine.

the sphere of perfect communion is clear everywhere
the pitcher water is alive, the willow eyes are green
there are also cold crags and early green bamboo
why are people these days in such a great hurry?

the cliffs are high and deep, the waters rush and tumble
the realm of perfect communion is new in each place
face to face, the people who meet her don't recognize her
when will they ever be free from the harbor of illusion?

lotus blossoms always in her hands, she stands alone,
magnificent
a boy comes to call
wordless, eyes resemble eyebrows
know that outside of joining the palms and bowing the head
how could this thing be explained to him?

. . . the dense crags jut forth precipitous
the waterfalls spew an azure loom
in each land, the sphere of perfect communion
those who go in are rare.

the clouds are thin, the river endless
the universal door appears without deception
questioning the boy, he doesn't yet know it exists
he went uselessly searching in the cold of the mist and waves
in a hundred cities.

THOMAS CLEARY (*trans. and ed.*)
The Original Face,
An Anthology of Rinzai Zen

DAKINI DAY

TWENTY-FIFTH DAY OF THE MONTH

THE BUDDHA IS THE GODDESS
THE GODDESS IS THE BUDDHA.

RICK FIELDS, ALLAN HUNT BADINER (*ed.*)
'The Meeting of the Buddha and the Goddess,' *Dharma Gaia*

ॐ

Transcendent wisdom is feminine. She is known as the mother of all the Buddhas, the womb of origination. The matrix of all being has to be known deeply – penetrated – before Buddhahood can be attained. In Tantric iconography, the embrace of male and female signifies the union of compassion (male) and wisdom (female). Transcendent wisdom is sheer limitlessness, so she can never be known through words or images. She can only be penetrated through direct realization of her essential nature – emptiness.

Dakini Day in the summer expresses the absolute feminine: not only the nurturing earth but also the penetrating light of a diamond-sharp, crystal-clear sky.

❀ THE PRAISE of perfect wisdom, which Shariputra sings to the Buddha, is an ode to the perfected feminine. "The Mystic Hymn to the Wisdom Mother" is part of the dramatic discourse on Transcendent Wisdom.

The perfection of wisdom is the state of all-knowledge ... The perfection of wisdom gives light ... She is worthy of homage. She is unstained and the entire world cannot stain her. She is a source of light and ... leads [everyone] away from the blinding darkness caused by defilement and wrong views. In her we can find shelter. Most excellent are her works. She makes us seek the safety of the wings of enlightenment ... She has gained the five eyes, and she shows the path to all beings. She herself is an organ of vision. She disperses the gloom and darkness of delusion ... She is the mother of the bodhisattvas ... She protects the unprotected ... She is the antidote to birth-and-death ... The perfection of wisdom of the Buddhas ... sets in motion the wheel of dharma.

EDWARD CONZE (*trans.*)
Ashtasahasrika VII,
Buddhist Texts through the Ages

✳ THE BODHISATTVA'S vow to benefit all beings eventually becomes a reality. Yeshe Tsogyal, who was the consort of Guru Padmasambhava in Tibet and the greatest wisdom dakini ever, describes her compassionate activity. The expression of wisdom is spontaneous compassion.

To those sentient beings who were hungry,
I manifested as an abundance of food,
establishing them in bliss.
To those sentient beings who were cold,
I manifested as sun and fire,
establishing them in bliss.

To those sentient beings who were poor,
I manifested as myriads of jewels,
establishing them in bliss.
To those sentient beings who lacked clothes,
I manifested as apparel,
establishing them in bliss.
To those sentient beings without children,
I manifested as sons and daughters,
establishing them in bliss.
To those sentient beings desiring a woman,
I manifested as an irresistible maiden,
establishing them in bliss.
To those sentient beings desiring a husband,
I manifested as a handsome man,
establishing them in bliss.

To those sentient beings wanting supernatural powers,
I gave the eight great siddhi practices,
establishing them in bliss.

To those sentient beings suffering from sickness,
I manifested as medicine,
establishing them in bliss.
To those sentient beings suffering from misery,
I manifested as satisfaction,
establishing them in bliss.

. . . To those sentient beings who were blind,
I manifested as eyes,
establishing them in bliss.
To those sentient beings who were crippled,
I manifested as limbs,
establishing them in bliss.
To those sentient beings who were dumb,
I manifested as tongues,
establishing them in bliss.

. . . In short, wherever there is space,
the five elements are pervasive.
Wherever there are the five elements,
sentient beings are pervasive.
Wherever there are sentient beings, emotions are pervasive.
Wherever there are emotions, my compassion is pervasive.
That is how widespread my help has been.

YESHE TSOGYAL, TARTHANG TULKU (*trans.*)
Mother of Knowledge

PROTECTOR DAY

TWENTY-NINTH DAY OF THE MONTH

**SOMETIMES TEACHING MUST BE STRONG.
COMPASSION IS NOT ONLY GENTLENESS. A SHARP
BLOW OF THE ... STICK OF AWAKENING, PLACED JUST RIGHT,
IS ALSO AN ACT OF COMPASSION.**

TAISEN DESHIMARU
The Ring of the Way

འ

The flowers of wisdom have tremendous variety. Some blooms are rare and exotic in unimaginable colors. Even black. The blossoming of wisdom – which penetrates the depths of reality to uncover no-thing-ness – releases the sublime energy of compassion. Not just the peaceful, loving, nurturing kind, but flaming, black, and wrathful. The later discourses of the Buddha that blossomed into the Great Way – the Mahayana – are dramatic dialogues involving gods, humans, nagas, bodhisattvas, and different manifestations of Buddhas, often in celestial realms inaccessible to ordinary perception. Among the many buddhas were awesomely fierce protectors enacting end-of-the-world cosmic rage, from the still center of all-seeing, all-knowing eyes.

ONE OF the foremost protectors or dharmapalas in Tibetan Buddhism is Mahakala – literally, Great Black One – whose fierce black form is encircled in flames. This excerpt is from a prayer to Mahakala.

Great mighty dharmapalas who come forth amidst roaring

flames of blessings and dark rolling clouds of thunder and lightning – surrounded

by your oceans of fierce emanations … immediately come enter this place …

Mahakala … and all you powerful protectors of the doctrine … accept these vast

cumulus clouds of … offerings which fill the whole of space …

Partake of them with delight! … please perform the four glorious activities:

Pacify all sickness, negative forces, and obstacles!

Enrich our lifespans, merit, glory, and wealth!

Magnetize the three worlds and the three realms of existence!

Destroy emnity and obstructing forces into dust!

Liberate craving, aggression and ignorance … Bless us! Remain always with us! Protect us …

Grant us the highest teachings and lead us on the path! … Give us long life and health …

and the increase of prosperity! … Remove all … obstacles! Subdue all demons, enemies and

vow breakers! … Empty the depths of samsara.

May there be no untimely death, illness … or obstructing spirits for us. May we have no

nightmares, ill omens or bad dealings. May the world enjoy peace, have good harvests,

abundant grain, expansion of dharma, and glorious auspiciousness.

Accomplish whatever mind desires.

Prayer to Mahakala

NEW MOON DAY

YOU SHOULD RATHER BE GRATEFUL FOR THE WEEDS YOU HAVE IN YOUR MIND, BECAUSE EVENTUALLY THEY WILL ENRICH YOUR PRACTICE.

SHUNRYU SUZUKI
Zen Mind, Beginner's Mind

ॐ

In the new moon of summer the noble aspiration of the bodhisattva, to rescue all beings from suffering, begins to take on a distinct form. Leaving the blissful land of silent light, the bodhisattva enters the confused world of ordinary beings, planting seeds of awareness, tending their delicate growth until they become trees of enlightenment. The heartwood or core of the tree of enlightenment is nondual wisdom. It's called emptiness because there is no essence, no self. When the heart is completely open, the phenomenal world is no longer divided into perceiver and object of perception.

Summer new moon is the time for the first courageous step toward ultimate wisdom – the gateless gate. It's a time for expanding, becoming courageous, walking the endless path with no object in mind whatsoever.

Bodhisattvas … leave the blissful land of silent light and come to the miserable world of five corruptions to make trees of enlightenment. High meadows on dry ground do not produce lotuses; it is the mud of the low swamps that gives birth to lotus blossoms. A farmer … cannot plant crops on clear dry ground – putting dirty manure into wet mud, he plants rice seeds there … sprouts grow, roots and stems, branches and leaves flourish … and grain ripens; when the farmer's work is done, he sings songs of peace and tranquility …

The appearance of buddhas in the world is also like this. In the … vastness of the sky you cannot construct a teaching of enlightenment, so they put on … ragged clothes … and guide sentient beings … by explaining the truth … planting seeds of the true basis…

People of the way are like a tree blood body; putting the manure of the six sense fields on the ground, planting the seeds of living awareness … sending forth shoots of inherent knowledge… bringing forth branches of conscious spirit … opening flowers of knowledge and vision, producing the fruit of enlightenment. When the work of the way is done, they sing the song of mindlessness.

Ordinary people are also like trees; on the thin soil of folly and delusion putting the manure of greed and lust, planting seeds of ignorance… growing roots of attachment and stems of the sense of others and self, bringing forth branches of flattery and deceit, sprouting leaves of jealousy and envy, creating trees of affliction, causing flowers of infatuation to bloom, farming fruits of the three poisons. When the tasks of fame and profit are done, they sing songs of desire.

Now tell me, are these three kinds of trees any better or worse than each other? If there is anyone who can pull them out by the roots with a single hand and plant them … where there is no light or shade and make a shadowless tree, he must be someone of great power, who has the same root as heaven and earth, the same body as myriad things. But tell me: who is this, what is he? If you say he is a Buddha, heaven and earth are far apart.

ZEN MASTER DAIKAKU, THOMAS CLEARY *(trans. and ed.)*
The Original Face, An Anthology of Rinzai Zen

❀ THICH NHAT HANH'S poem shows the joy of walking the bodhisattva path with the wisdom of nonduality.

Peace is every step.
The shining red sun is my heart.
Each flower smiles with me.
How green, how fresh all that grows.
How cool the wind blows.
Peace is every step.
It turns the endless path to joy.

THICH NHAT HANH
Peace Is Every Step

TURNING
OF THE WHEEL

FESTIVAL DAY ~ FULL MOON DAY IN JULY

THE BEST OF PATHS IS THE PATH OF EIGHT. THE BEST OF TRUTHS, THE FOUR SAYINGS; THE BEST OF STATES, FREEDOM FROM PASSIONS; THE BEST OF MEN, THE ONE WHO SEES.

The Dhammapada

After the Buddha became enlightened, he stayed in silent meditation for seven weeks. He had reached the ultimate truth, but how could it be communicated? The god Brahma begged him to turn the wheel of dharma. But who was ready to hear it? With his divine eye he saw the group of five ascetics who had attended him on the path. They were living at the Deer Park near Benares. The first turning of the wheel of dharma marks the third extraordinary day in the Buddhist year.

❋ IN THE first cycle of teaching the dharma, the Buddha taught the four noble truths and the eight-fold path.

When friends, a noble disciple understands suffering, the cessation of suffering, and the way leading to the cessation of suffering, in that way he is one of right view ... and has arrived at the true Dharma.

Birth is suffering ... Ageing ... sickness ... death ... sorrow, lamentation, pain, grief, and despair are suffering; not to obtain what one wants is suffering ...

And what is the origin of suffering? It is craving, which brings renewal of being, is accompanied by delight and lust ... craving for sensual pleasures, craving for being, and ... for nonbeing. This is called the origin of suffering.

And what is the cessation of suffering? It is ... giving up, letting go, and rejecting that same craving ...

And what is the way leading to the cessation of suffering? It is just this Noble Eightfold Path; that is, right view, right thought, right speech, right action, right livelihood, right effort, right mindfulness, right concentration.

BHIKKU NANAMOLI (*trans.*)
The Middle Length Discourses of the Buddha

❋ AMONG THE Buddha's first teachings is a description of the beginningless cycle of samsara, or worldly existence, based on ignorance and perpetuated by desire or craving. The point of this somewhat stark portrayal is to show the way out.

Incalculable, brethren, is the beginning of this round of rebirth. No beginning is made known of beings wrapt in ignorance, fettered by craving, who run on … the round of rebirth.

There comes a time … when the mighty ocean dries up, is utterly drained, comes no more to be. But of beings hindered in ignorance, fettered by craving, who run on … I declare no end-making.

Just as … a dog tied up by a leash to a strong stake or pillar keeps … revolving round … even so [those] who … regard body as the self … regard consciousness as having a self … or the self as being in consciousness … revolve … from body to body … they are not released … from rebirth, old age and decay … from suffering …

But the noble well-taught disciple … who … regards no body as the self, regards not the self as being in consciousness … revolves not from body to body … from consciousness to consciousness, but is released from there.

He is released from birth, old age and decay, from sorrow and grief, woe, lamentation and despair.

L. FREER (*ed.*)
Samyutta Nikaya, vol. iii

❋ THE BUDDHA was insistent that the dharma was not a belief system, a catechism. The point was to experience the truth for oneself. Blind faith is not the way.

Monks and scholars should
Analyze my words as one would analyze gold
Through melting, refining, and polishing,
And adopt them only then –
Not for the sake of showing me respect.

GESHE WANGYAL in
The Jewelled Staircase

BIRTHDAY OF THE SEVENTEENTH KARMAPA

TWENTY-SIXTH DAY OF JUNE

THE KARMAPAS ARE RENOWNED AS THE BLACK HAT LAMAS OF TIBET, THE BLACK CROWN SIGNIFYING THEIR SPIRITUAL MASTERY. THE SEVENTEENTH LIVING BUDDHA IN THIS SUPREME LINEAGE WAS BORN IN TIBET ON 26 JUNE 1985 AMIDST WONDROUS SIGNS.

The Buddha predicted that sixteen hundred years after his passing there would come a man of perfect wisdom and infinite compassion, who would take human form twenty-one times to spread the Buddhist teaching. He would be known as Karmapa, possessor or master of activity.

The feats of the Karmapas became legendary. Marco Polo recorded the miracles of the second Karmapa at the court of the Chinese emperor. One hundred and fifty years later, the emperor, T'ai Ming Chen, presented the Black Crown to the fifth Karmapa to acknowledge his spiritual mastery. From that time the Karmapas were renowned as the Black Hat Lamas of Tibet. For three hundred years they were gurus to the emperors of China.

The system for maintaining this lineage of living Buddhas depends on the power of each Karmapa to recognize his successor. Accordingly, before the sixteenth Karmapa died in 1981, he wrote a letter predicting where he would be reborn and to whom. He gave it to his intimate disciple, Tai Situpa, who is himself the twelfth master in a lineage of supreme incarnations. The letter was wrapped in a piece of clothing disguised as a protection amulet. Karmapa handed it to him saying, "This is protection for you and in the future it will be very beneficial." Searching everywhere for the prediction instructions, Tai Situpa decided to look inside the amulet in 1989 and found the letter. It said the father of the next Karmapa was called Dondrup, the mother was Logala, and that they lived in a nomad's place "with the sign of the cow" in east Tibet. The child's birthday was "in the year of the one used for the earth," and he would be born "with the miraculous, far-reaching sound of the white one." When the search party arrived at Bakor ("the sign of the cow") in the Lhatok region of east Tibet, the place matched a vision of the Dalai Lama in which he saw the Karmapa's birthplace. There, in the year of the wood ox ("the one used for the earth"), a special son had been born to nomad parents Dondrup and Logala. The villagers all said they heard celestial music for three days after his birth. The "miraculous far-reaching sound" of the conch shell had filled the skies.

The child was ready when the search party arrived in Bakor. He had insisted that the family move one month early from their winter encampment to the summer one – so that he would be found according to the prediction letter. When he heard some monks were looking for the seventeenth Karmapa, he became very excited. "My monks are coming. I'm going to my monastery," he said.

In September, 1992, the seventeenth Karmapa was enthroned at Tsurphu, seat of the Karmapas in central Tibet. The ceremony, performed by Tai Situpa, was attended by Chinese officials – who accorded unprecedented approval to the "Living Buddha" – forty thousand Tibetans including many senior Lamas, and international devotees. He was named Urgyen Drodul Trinley Dorje, "Indestructible Buddha Activity, the Tamer of Living Beings from Oddiyana."

The Times Saturday Review 5 December 1992: 'A Star is Raised and Borne'

Tai Situpa wrote this poem to honor the birth of the seventeenth Karmapa.

In the spaciousness of the great expanse, the universal matrix,
The planets dance unhindered.
The indestructible diamond of self-liberating reality
Is the changeless absolute nature.

Urgyen, sprout of the Victorious Ones,
Diamond scepter of the enlightened activity to train beings,
Embodiment of all-pervading primordial awareness
*   You are the one who leads to total victory in every direction.*

TAI SITUPA

BIRTHDAY OF
THE DALAI LAMA

SIXTH DAY OF JULY

THE DALAI LAMA IS THE SPIRITUAL AND POLITICAL LEADER OF THE TIBETAN PEOPLE.

HE HAS BEEN PERHAPS THE MOST INFLUENTIAL FIGURE IN POPULARIZING

TIBETAN BUDDHISM.

The present Dalai Lama was born into a peasant family in the eastern Tibetan province of Amdo in 1935 and is the fourteenth in the succession of Dalai Lamas. *Dalai* is a title of Mongolian origin and means "ocean," implying a vast repository of wisdom. The title was first bestowed in 1642 on the Fifth Dalai Lama (the previous four were recognized posthumously) by Gusri Khan, one of the new generation of Mongol Khans. He installed the Fifth

Detail of TIBETAN TANGKA OF THE DALAI LAMA

Dalai Lama as virtual ruler of Tibet under Mongolian protection. And so the institution of spiritual and political leader remained, until the Chinese invasion of 1950.

The Dalai Lamas, like all the great lineages of Tibetan Buddhism, are tulkus, which means they are bodhisattvas in a lineage of recognized reincarnations. The recognition is entirely spiritual, based on oracular prophesies, visions, and memory tests. So a tulku can be born in any race, ethnic group, or social class.

The present Dalai Lama frequently emphasizes that he is a simple monk. He is considered one of the great Dalai Lamas – the others being the Fifth and the Thirteenth – and is venerated not only by all Tibetans but also by an increasing number of Western disciples. His status as a world spiritual leader was recognized in 1992 when he was awarded the Nobel Peace Prize. Because of the near-mythic status of the "God-Kings of Tibet," and equally his own charisma, the Dalai Lama has perhaps been the most influential figure in popularizing Tibetan Buddhism.

Developing a kind heart is not just for people who believe in religion … It is for anybody who considers himself to be a member of the human family.

THE FOURTEENTH DALAI LAMA
Mind Science

My belief may be too simple, but I feel that from birth to death affection is the most important basis for the existence of all sentient beings, particularly humans … Some medical scientists say that the first few weeks following birth are a crucial period for the growth of the brain and that physical touch … is vital for the healthy development of the baby's brain. So just as a flower needs the right temperature and moisture to grow properly, human beings need the warmth of affection for … their physical body to develop properly.

THE FOURTEENTH DALAI LAMA
Mind Science

ANNIVERSARY OF ACHAAN BUDDHADASA

EIGHTH DAY OF JULY

ACHAAN BUDDHADASA (1906–1993) IS KNOWN FOR HIS SCIENTIFIC, STRAIGHTFORWARD, AND PRACTICAL APPROACH TO THE BUDDHA'S TEACHING. HE ESTABLISHED SUAN MOKH, A FOREST MEDITATION CENTER IN THAILAND, AND WORKED WITH OTHER RELIGIONS FOR WORLD PEACE.

༄

Buddhadasa – literally "Slave of the Buddha" – continues to be the best-known dharma teacher in Thailand. He became a monk at the age of twenty and, after completing his studies, went into retreat in the forest to be close to nature like the Buddha. He avoided all human contact for six years and then established Suan Mokh (The Garden of the Power of Liberation), a forest meditation center. His approach to the Buddha's teachings was considered scientific, straightforward, and practical, emphasizing meditation in daily life, and the real chance of attaining nirvana "here and now." His teaching influenced education, social work, and rural development and inspired a new generation of socially concerned monks. He studied all the Buddhist schools and major religions in order to work together with everyone for world peace. One of the many projects he established was "Dharma Mothers" to develop women teachers of the dharma.

Detail from Arearea
PAUL GAUGUIN 1848–1903

✻ BUDDHADASA EMPHASIZED that the heart of Buddhism was the Buddha's teaching: "Nothing whatsoever should be clung to." He explained that birth meant the emergence of clinging to "I" and "mine"; and that if one stopped clinging, one automatically stopped birth and attained nirvana – the unborn, which does not age, sicken, or die. In 1987, Buddhadasa wrote this poem:

Buddhadasa will never die.
Even when the body dies, it will not listen
whether it is or is not, is of no consequence,
it is only something passing through time.

Buddhadasa carries on, there's no dying.
However good or bad the times
one with the true teaching.
Having offered body and mind in ceaseless service
under Lord Buddha's command.

Buddhadasa lives on, there's no dying.
In service to all humanity forever
through the Dharma proclamations left behind –
O Friends, can't you see! What dies?

Even when I die and the body ceases
my voice still echoes in comrades' ears
clear and bright, as loud as ever.
Just as if I never died
the Dharma-body lives on.

Treat me as if I never died,
as though I am with you all as before.
Speak up whatever is on your minds
as if I sit with you helping point out the facts.

Treat me as if I never died,
then many streams of benefits will accrue.
… Realize the absolute and stop dying.

ACHAAN BUDDHADASA
Heartwood of the Bodhi Tree

ANNIVERSARY OF NAGARJUNA

TWENTY-EIGHTH DAY OF JULY

NAGARJUNA WAS AN INDIAN ADEPT, SCHOLAR AND PHYSICIAN

WHO ESTABLISHED THE PHILOSOPHICAL SCHOOL KNOWN AS THE MIDDLE WAY.

Four hundred years after the Buddha passed away, there appeared a great adept whose heroic spiritual activity firmly established the path to transcendent wisdom, thus liberating countless disciples and promulgating the Mahayana, or Great Way. He came to be known as Nagarjuna. His appearance was predicted by the Buddha.

After I, the Buddha, have passed away,
Four hundred years will elapse,
And then a monk called Naga will appear.
He will be devoted to the Doctrine
And be of great benefit to it.
He will attain the stage of Perfect Bliss,
Live for six hundred years,
And will secure the mystic knowledge
Of the Mahamyuri Tantra.
He will know the subjects of the different sciences,
And expound the teaching of nonsubstantiality,
And after he has cast away his bodily frame,
He will be reborn in the region of Sukhavati,
And finally, he will attain Buddhahood.

TARTHANG TULKU
Manjushri-mala-tantra,
Crystal Mirror, vol. V

❋ ACCORDING TO one biographer, Nagarjuna first sought instruction in medicine from Guru Padmasambhava (who was residing in a nearby cemetery) in order to win a contest with his stepbrother for his father's throne. He won but had no interest in worldly power and continued studying with the Guru.

Some years later, all eighty-four temples of Vikramasila monastery were incinerated by a magically produced flame, thus destroying three-quarters of all Buddhist scriptures. The Naga king living in the ocean became extremely ill from the smoke and the Great Doctor was summoned. The treatment worked. To show his gratitude, the Naga king revealed the great treasury of the Prajnaparamita Sutra, with which he had been entrusted by the Buddha's disciple Ananda. That's how Nagarjuna got his name – holder of great power in the Naga realm.

Nagarjuna spent fifty years studying the texts and then promulgated them throughout India. The philosophical school that Nagarjuna established came to be known as the Madhyamika, the middle way between the two extremes of eternalism – the belief that a self exists – and nihilism – the belief in no-self. The middle way neither asserts nor denies. It is "formless, undemonstrable, unsupported, nonmanifesting, without designation and situation." (Candrakirti).

I bow before that Nagarjuna who has rejected
The adherence to the two extreme points of view …
The fires of his doctrine consume the fuel
Of every contradictory, conflicting view;
While its brilliance dispels until this very day
The mental darkness of the entire world.
His incomparable wisdom and words …
Secure for him sovereignty over the three spheres of existence,
… And vanquish the host of enemies – the hosts of Phenomenal Existence.

CANDRAKIRTI
Crystal Mirror, vol. V

FRUITION

AUTUMN

Fruition in the Buddhist path is called realization. When subject and object are no longer polarized, impure phenomenal appearance is understood to be none other than the play of Buddha-mind that pervades all of space.

With moral conduct and mindfulness as the basis, and aspiration to benefit others as motivation, it is possible to transform gross body elements into subtle energy and habitual karmic patterns into pristine awareness. Extracting weeds by the root, cultivating the flower of experience, the nondual state of bliss and emptiness arises. The autumn harvest is abundant with blessing.

The maturation of experience is like alchemy. Cultivating with awareness rather than abandoning with disgust the objects of sensual pleasure, they transform into their true nature. "Sow the seeds, ripen the fruit, refine the fluid and the essence emerges," said Milarepa. Refinement is an alchemical process using the subtle energy channels of the mind-body to become a Buddha in one lifetime.

If you wish to realize the essence of mind,
You should practice the following teachings:
Faith, knowledge, and discipline,
These three are the life-tree of mind,
This is the tree you should plant and foster.

. . . Meditation, diligence, and perseverance,
These three are the horses of mind;
They run fast and quickly flee!
If you look for horses, these are the right ones.

Self-awareness, self-illumination, and self-rapture,
These three are the fruits of mind.
Sow the seeds, ripen the fruit,
Refine the fluid, and the essence emerges.
If you look for fruit, these are the fruit you should seek.

GARMA C.C. CHANG (*trans.*)
The Hundred Thousand Songs of Milarepa

Tibetan yogis, like Milarepa, were able to demonstrate miracles as the fruit or result of their practice. Harnessing the subtle energies of the body-mind, they could fly in the sky, walk through rocks, sit on blades of grass, and ride on sunbeams. These siddhis, or powers, were the result of the very special methods of the Tantric path, brought from India to Tibet by the Tantric Buddha, Padmasambhava. Tantra means continuity or continuum. And Buddha-nature is the deepest, purest foundation of all being. It is continuous, here and now. Samsara and nirvana are inseparable. That being the case, the most direct route to realization – for the mature and well-prepared practitioner – is through the objects of the senses and the raw energy of the emotions.

The great wisdom dakini Yeshe Tsogyal pointed out the Tantric path to countless disciples.

> *If you cut away the root, the one mind itself will arise from within*
> *and pervade all the "outside" with great Pristine Awareness.*
> *Innate bliss will whirl like the ocean,*
> *and insight will penetrate like the golden eye of the great fish.*
>
> *Use and guard this deep experience and bliss;*
> *leap beyond and through to perfect creativity;*
> *run and roll through the fields of appearance;*
> *disappear and fly up into space.*
>
> *In the broad expanse of great Pristine Awareness merge into the ocean of the nectar of Great Bliss.*
>
> NAMKHAI NYINGPO, TARTHANG TULKU (*trans.*)
> *Mother of Knowledge*

The Buddha taught many different methods for psychologically different types of people. For some people, it was appropriate to cut off sexual desire, for example, by meditating on the impurity of the body until disgust arose. Another kind of person could look at the object of desire very deeply until its illusory nature became apparent. People with strong passions but disciplined, mature, and tamed, could take desire itself as the path, and transform it. This is the Tantric way. These different methods are not necessarily mutually exclusive but describe stages of spiritual development. A yogi would practice all three. As the Tibetan Buddhist master Tarthang Tulku puts it, "Tantra refers primarily to one's individual growth and only secondarily to the body of literature which deals with this developmental process" *(Crystal Mirror)*. Just as the arhat, or solitary realizer, is the ideal of the first type of path, and the bodhisattva the ideal of the second, so the yogi, or adept, is the hero of Tantra.

Tantric wisdom is often esoteric, symbolic, elaborate, and devotional. The guru is the Buddha; realizing this, one receives the blessing of the Buddha. Devotion thus sets in motion a process of transformation whereby the phenomenal world becomes sacred.

The fourth major event in the Buddhist calendar celebrates the Buddha's descent from the realm of the heavenly gods to the human realm. Prince Siddhartha's mother died seven days after giving birth to the son destined to be the Buddha. According to the sutras, she was reborn in the realm of the heavenly gods. To repay her kindness, liberate her, and benefit the gods, the Buddha spent three months teaching in the god realms. The descent to the human realms is celebrated at the end of November.

MEDICINE BUDDHA DAY

EIGHTH DAY OF THE MONTH

BIRTH, LIFE AND DEATH HAVE LOST THEIR HOLD
UPON THIS MADMAN ...
MEDITATION UPON THE UNOBSTRUCTED SENSE FIELDS
IS PURE PLEASURE ...

KEITH DOWMAN (*trans.*)
Masters of Enchantment

Meditation on impermanence and death naturally leads to the understanding that the dharma is the supreme medicine for all the mind's ills. However, the Tantric path in particular uses a more holistic approach to medicine. What are usually seen as poisons – the sense pleasures – are prescribed for the wise who can transform them into nectar. Tantric Buddhism works on the same principle as alchemy, turning base metals into gold. But it comes strictly on prescription, with the instructions of a qualified guru.

❋ THIS POIGNANT poem captures the landscape of autumn and the chill wind of change. The only cure for death is the dharma – realizing that there is no self to die.

In spring, the season of warmth and growth,
The stalks of the crops were turquoise green,
Now, autumn's end, the fields lie naked and parched,
My mind turns to thoughts of my death.

On each branch of the trees in my garden
Hang clusters of fruit, swelling and ripe,
In the end, not one piece will remain.
My mind turns to thoughts of my death.

From behind the peaks of Mount Potala
The sun rose like an umbrella in the sky.
Now it has gone, fallen behind the western ranges,
My mind turns to thoughts of my death.

. . . Gray clouds cover the sky, obscuring it;
The first drops of rain are about to fall,
To be scattered everywhere by the dark, red wind.
My mind turns to thoughts of my death.

. . . Warm summer days, the earth thronging with life;
The minds of the people are lost in gaiety.
Suddenly the cold winter wind crashes them down.
My mind turns to thoughts of my death.

High above turquoise dragons roared in harmony;
Around me cuckoo birds chattered sweetly.
But times have changed; where are they now?
My mind turns to thoughts of my death.

Dharma, the precious teachings of the Awakened Ones,
Is a medicine supreme, curing all the mind's ills.
These days many saints of old look down from Pure Lands.
My mind turns to thoughts of my death.

THE SEVENTH DALAI LAMA, GLENN H. MULLIN (*trans.*)
Selected Works of the Dalai Lama VII:
Songs of Spiritual Change

❋ IN INDIA, the practice of Tantric Buddhism, which developed meditation techniques attuned to the work routines of everyday life, resulted in mahasiddhas, men of great miraculous powers. Sense pleasures become the fastest path to liberation.

One of the greatest mahasiddhas was Saraha, whose guru was Rahula, the Buddha's son. His poem "The Royal Song of Saraha" is a brilliant exposition of the Tantric Buddhist view and methods. One simple stanza emphasizes compassionate motivation as the basis for alchemical transformation.

Like salt sea water that turns
Sweet when drunk up by the clouds,
So a firm mind that works for others turns
The poison of sense-objects into nectar.

LONGCHENPA,
HERBERT GUENTHER (*trans.*)
A Visionary Journey

❋ THE PRINCIPLE of transformation is to understand that both positive and negative have the same essence. The wise know this, but the foolish get lost in the five poisonous emotions: ignorance, jealousy, attachment, hatred, and pride.

While medicine heals and poison kills,
Their ultimate essence is the same.
Both positive and negative qualities
Are aids on the path –
The sage rejects nothing.
Yet the unrealized fool
Five times poisoned
Is lost forever in samsara.

KEITH DOWMAN (*trans.*)
Masters of Enchantment

PADMASAMBHAVA DAY

TENTH DAY OF THE MONTH

**THE TRUE-NATURE IS EXTREMELY PROFOUND,
EXCEEDINGLY SUBTLE AND SUBLIME.
IT DOES NOT ATTACH TO SELF-NATURE,
BUT MANIFESTS FOLLOWING (CAUSAL) CONDITIONS.**

UISANG
Ocean Seal of Huayen Buddhism, *Process Metaphysics and Hua Yen Buddhism*

The transformation of nature is more apparent in the autumn than at any other time of the year. Padmasambhava Day in October celebrates the transformation of time itself. Padmasambhava, while disputing with a sect known as the Tirthikas, was offered a poisoned drink. He turned it into nectar and inspired their faith in him. At the same time he transformed into a yogi known as Nyima Oser, who is depicted using the rays of the sun to hold it still. This shows his mastery of time – day and night, and the four seasons. So Padmasambhava Day in the autumn penetrates the natural cycle itself.

✳ CONTEMPORARY TIBETAN master Chogyam Trungpa explains how the four seasons give us a natural sense of security, of belonging, and why this comfort zone has to be punctured in order to relate directly with the truth.

Usually day and night and the four seasons bring us comfort by giving us the feeling we are relating with reality, with the elements: "Now we are relating with summer ... with autumn ... with winter, and ... with spring. How good to be alive! How good to be on earth, man's best place, his home! It's getting late; it's time for dinner. We could begin the day with a hearty breakfast." And so forth. Our lifestyle is governed by these concepts. There are lots of things to do as time goes along, and relating with them is like swinging in a hammock, a comfortable bed in the open air. But Nyima Oser punctured this hammock. Now you can't have a good time swinging and having a comfortable snooze in the open air. That's the penetrating quality here.

CHOGYAM TRUNGPA
Crazy Wisdom

✳ CHOGYAM TRUNGPA'S poem expresses the ecstatic joy of yogic transformation of the elements and mastery of phenomena. Tantric mystic poetry is esoteric superrealism, exuberant and awesome.

Dancing in space,
Clad in clouds,
Eating the sun and holding the moon,
The stars are my retinue.

The naked child is beautiful and dignified.
The red flower blooms in the sky.
It is ironic to see the formless dancer,
Dancing to the trumpet without a trumpeter.

At the palace of red ruby,
Listening to the utterance of the seed syllable,
It is joyful to watch the dance of illusion,
The seductive maidens of phenomena.

The warrior without a sword,
Riding on a rainbow,
Hears the limitless laughter of transcendent joy,
The poisonous snake becomes amrita.

Drinking fire, wearing water,
Holding the mace of the wind,
Breathing earth,
I am the lord of the three worlds.

CHOGYAM TRUNGPA
Enthronement, *The Myth of Freedom*

FULL MOON DAY

FIFTEENTH DAY OF THE MONTH

SIXTY-SIX TIMES HAVE THESE EYES BEHELD THE CHANGING SCENES OF AUTUMN.

I HAVE SAID ENOUGH ABOUT MOONLIGHT; ASK ME NO MORE.

ONLY LISTEN TO THE VOICE OF PINES AND CEDARS WHEN NO WIND STIRS.

JOSEPH GOLDSTEIN
The Experience of Insight

In the autumn, the fruit of the tree of wisdom is ripe. Wisdom-fruit has many flavors, some exotic and pungent, others subtle and refined right to the very core.

In the Tantric path, wisdom is born from supplicating the guru with unfabricated longing, thus creating the space for a mind-to-mind transmission. The deep yearning of devotion engenders vibrant creativity, known as miracles. Devotion brings the rain of the guru's blessing, which falls on the seeds inherent in the mind-ground, flowering into wisdom and bearing the fruit of enlightenment.

The Mind-ground holds the seeds
Which sprout when falls the all-pervading rain.
The wisdom flower of instantaneous awakening
Cannot fail to bear the Bodhi-fruit.

LU KUAN YU (*trans.*)
The Transmission of Mind

⁂ THROUGH THE blessings of the guru, devotion ripens into wisdom that sees the rootless, ultimate nature of everything.

The autumn sky sparklingly clear
Was not by any man polished so fair;
When from transient shadows it is free,
Indeed it is a delight to the eye.
    The rootless, ultimate nature of things
    Is not the creation of a recent thinker;
    When at last highest truth is known,
    False essence fades into itself and is gone.

The rainbow with its radiance and play
Has no basis on which to rely;
From conditions and the workings of lights
Magically spring fire so bright.
    The things that appear outside and in
    Have no self-nature to reveal.
    From the fantasies of an ill-taught mind,
    We know a reality with false images entwined.

THE SEVENTH DALAI LAMA, GLENN H. MULLIN (*trans.*)
Selected Works of the Dalai Lama VII:
Songs of Spiritual Change

❁ FRUITION EXPRESSED in the Zen path is like looking into absolutely clear, pure water to the very depths of the ocean. When the depths of the mind have been penetrated, emotional turbulence is like the reflection of moonlight on waves.

Spotless, the moonlight reflected
In the waters of the mind.
Even the waves break against it
And shatter into light.

TAISEN DESHIMARU
The Ring of the Way

❁ THE THERAVADIN expression of fruition is not to separate an experiencer from the experience.

People ask, "Are you an arhat (one who has reached a high stage of spiritual progress)?" Do I know? I am like a tree, full of leaves, blossoms and fruit. Birds come to eat and nest. Yet the tree does not know itself. It follows its nature; it is as it is.

ACHAAN CHAH,
JACK KORNFIELD AND PAUL BREITER (comp. and ed.)
A Still Forest Pool

❁ AUTUMN IS the time for collecting the ripened fruit of the tree of wisdom.

When you have wisdom, contact with sense objects, whether good or bad, pleasant or painful, is like standing at the bottom of a mango tree and collecting the fruit while another person climbs up and shakes it down for us. We get to choose between the good and rotten mangoes, and we do not have to waste our strength because we do not have to climb up the tree.

What does this mean? All the sense objects that come to us are bringing us knowledge. We do not need to embellish them. The eight worldly winds – gain and loss, fame and disrepute, praise and blame, pain and pleasure – come of their own. If your heart has developed tranquility and wisdom, you can enjoy picking and choosing. What others may call good or bad, here or there, happiness or suffering, is all to your profit, because someone else has climbed up to shake the mangoes down, and you have nothing to fear.

The eight worldly winds are like mangoes falling down to you. Use your concentration and tranquility to contemplate, to collect. Knowing which fruits are good and which are rotten is called wisdom … If there is wisdom, insight arises naturally. Although I call it wisdom, you do not have to give it a name.

ACHAAN CHAH,
JACK KORNFIELD AND PAUL BREITER (comp. and ed.)
A Still Forest Pool

DAKINI DAY

IN THE THREE WORLDS, THERE IS NO GREATER SIN THAN TO BE WITHOUT LOVE. THEREFORE, YOU MUST NEVER BE WITHOUT IT.

HERBERT GUENTHER (*trans.*)
The Life and Teaching of Naropa

ॐ

In Tantric Buddhism, women are exalted. One of the important Tantric vows – especially for male practitioners – is never to disparage women. The Candamaharosana Tantra cautions:

One should honour women.
Women are heaven, women are truth,
Women are the supreme fire of transformation.
Women are Buddha, women are religious community.
Women are the perfection of wisdom.

MIRANDA SHAW
Passionate Enlightenment

※ IN TANTRIC Buddhism, none of the sense pleasures are rejected. The meditation invoking great bliss in sexual union is the "lower gate" to enlightenment. Padmasambhava, the Tantric Buddha, makes a very clear statement regarding the importance of Tantric union.

I myself am unsullied by desire or lust;
and such faults as attachment do not exist in me.
But a woman is a necessary accouterment to the secret
teachings:

. . . Without such a one,
the maturation and liberation practices are obstructed.
The result, the achievement of the secret teachings
does not occur.

TARTHANG TULKU (*trans.*)
Mother of Knowledge

❋ ONCE WHEN the great dakini, Yeshe Tsogyal, was in a remote area of Tibet, seven bandits wanted to rape her and steal her possessions. But at the moment of sexual intercourse, she sang a song of secret Tantric instruction, pointing out how to "join with the space of the Mother's mandala" to realize great bliss. The Song of the Four Joys expresses the esoteric mudra or gesture of sexuality, in which the tightness of desire is released into the creative expanse. Turning obstacles into the path is the profound meaning of Tantra or "continuity." The result is the realization of Mahamudra, literally the great gesture.

... Today my sons, you meet with me, the Great Mother –
this is due to the power of merit gained before.
Now is the time – the conditions are right for the Four
Empowerments.
Listen, my sons, and be attentive;
I will move with you through the Four Joys.

Gazing upon the mandala of the Mother,
you will clearly see the feeling of desire arising,
... Explore the pure fact of your own desire –
merge inseparably with the deities ...
contemplate your desire mind as the deities' manifestation, my
sons.

Join with the space of the Mother's mandala;
Great Bliss arises from that root.
Pacify the angry mind; the loving mind replaces it,

and power is gained from the Secret Empowerment.
Explore the pure fact of joy –
merge joy with breath and let them circulate a little.
There is no turning back from the Mahamudra.
Explore the bliss of Mahamudra, my sons.

Join with the expanse of the Mother's Great Bliss.
Let your vigor take on a life of its own;
you and I will merge hearts and minds,
and gain blessing from the Wisdom Empowerment.
Guard unwavering the pure fact of bliss –
merge with the great Bliss which is openness.
Explore the Bliss of Supreme Joy, my sons.

Join with the root of the Mother's Bliss –
make the "two" of duality the "one" of enlightened mind.
Stop the appearance of self and others,
and gain Pristine Awareness from the Creativity
Empowerment.
Guard its spontaneity within the world of appearance.
Merge masterful desire with openness,
and there is no turning back from the Great Perfection.
Then explore transcending the Joy of Spontaneity, my sons.

These instructions are especially sublime.
Thus wondrous liberation comes from our meeting,
and instantly, with lightning speed,
you receive the Four Empowerments,
and reach maturity by realizing the Four Joys.

TARTHANG TULKU (*trans.*)
Mother of Knowledge

PROTECTOR DAY

TWENTY-NINTH DAY OF THE MONTH

**...FOR ALL BEINGS WHO HAVE BEEN WANDERING
COUNTLESS NUMBERS OF TIMES IN ENDLESS SAMSARA
AND WHO ENDURE UNBEARABLE TORMENTS,
THERE IS NO OTHER REFUGE THAN YOU, GREAT PROTECTOR.**

Prayer to the Protector Chenresig

In the yogic path, inner obstacles to transformation often appear outwardly as demons. The yogi has to realize that these are the negative projections of his or her own mind. So Protector Day in the autumn shows liberation from the worldly belief system of good and evil, the continuous battle played out between the forces of light and the forces of darkness. In fact, there is nothing that is static, immovable, everlasting. Penetrating the essence of both good and evil – the pure energy of Buddha-nature – the yogi turns obstacles into the path.

*Statue of the goddess Kwan Yin
Buddhist monastery-temple, Penang, Malaysia*

WHEN TIBET'S great yogi Milarepa meditated in solitude, he frequently encountered demons who tried to disturb his meditation. Understanding them to be "adornments" of his practice rather than obstacles, he sang this song:

You mischievous demons here assembled,
Lend your ears and listen closely to my song.

…From the great ocean vapors rise,
Reaching the vast sky.
They form great clouds;
A causal law governs the transformation of the elements.

In midsummer, rainbows appear above the plain,
Gently resting upon the hills.
Of the plains and mountains,
The rainbow is the beauty and adornment.

In the West, when rain falls in the cold ocean,
Bushes and trees flourish on the earth.
To all creatures on the Continent,
These are the beauty and adornment.

I, the yogi who desires to remain in solitude,
Meditate on the Voidness of Mind.
Awed by the power of my concentration,
You jealous demons are forced to practice magic.
Of the yogi, demonic conjurations
Are the beauty and adornment.

GARMA C.C. CHANG (*trans.*)
The Hundred Thousand Songs of Milarepa

AT ANOTHER time, when Milarepa was meditating on Mount Everest, he was attacked by the mountain goddess, Tserinma, who later became his consort. He sang her this song:

The malignant male and female demons
Who create myriad troubles and obstructions,
Seem real before one has Enlightenment;
But when one realizes their nature truly,
They become Protectors to the Dharma,
And by their help and (freely-given) assistance
One attains to numerous accomplishments.

… In time past, wrapped up in clinging blindness,
I lingered in the den of confusion,
Deeming benevolent deities and malignant
Demons to be real and subsistent …

Realizing the groundless nature of ignorance,
My former awareness, clouded and unstable
Like reflections of the moon in rippling water,
Becomes transparent, clear as shining crystal.
Its sunlike brilliance is free from obscuring clouds,
Its light transcends all forms of blindness,
Ignorance and confusion thus vanish without trace.
This is the truth I have experienced within.

GARMA C. C. CHANG (*trans.*)
The Hundred Thousand Songs of Milarepa

NEW MOON DAY

THIRTIETH DAY OF THE MONTH

**WHEN YOU DO SOMETHING, YOU SHOULD BURN
YOURSELF COMPLETELY, LIKE A GOOD BONFIRE,
LEAVING NO TRACE OF ITSELF.**

SHUNRYU SUZUKI
Zen Mind, Beginner's Mind

The most powerful experiences we have as human beings occur just before, and right after death. These experiences offer a unique opportunity for enlightenment.

All the Buddhist traditions emphasize constant awareness of impermanence and death. Autumn new moon looks squarely into the jaws of death, seeing it in the changing shades of the falling leaves, the sounds of the wild geese, the shortening days, and the onset of night. Looking directly at nostalgia and longing, youth and old age, birth and death, autumn becomes a profound meditation.

❋ THESE POEMS speak directly from the heart, telling of life's impermanence.

*Across the bank, maples have spread silken cloth,
The leaves are busy sprinkling autumn into the yard.
A wild goose screams onto the edge of the sky.
The night churns up a longing for home.*

JAIHIUN KIM (*comp. and trans.*)
Poems by Zen Masters

*The rain sounds, friendly pattering
on the bamboos which encircle the eaves.
Suffused with autumn colors,
the maples fill up every valley.
The yellow flowers are beautiful, glistening
tearlike in the dewdrops at dawn.
Off the trees the red-tinted leaves
start to fall into the yard.*

JAIHIUN KIM (*comp. and trans.*)
Poems by Zen Masters

*Life is impermanent like the setting sun,
Wealth is like dew on the morning grass,
Praise is like wind in a mountain pass,
A youthful body is an autumn flower.*

THE SEVENTH DALAI LAMA, GLENN H. MULLIN (*trans.*)
*Selected Works of the Dalai Lama VII:
Songs of Spiritual Change*

HERE IS a Western Buddhist's perspective of
those randomly falling leaves during
"Autumn Days in Zen Center."

Brown leaves swirling in the concrete yard,
Tossing and turning in forgotten moorings,
Clashing and colliding with other vestiges
Of organic existence,
The random rhythm of a disorderly dance.

Heavy skies, lashing winds in orderly garden,
With its pristine precision of weedless existence,
Rose bushes neatly nipped and clipped,
Strategic positions in black earth and full bloom.
Clean cut garden with unfrayed edges.

Leaves flying down to concrete squares
Erstwhile contribution to stable contrasts,
Homeless leaves in freefall,
Air to ground movers, uplifting, downplaying
In the force of circumstances.

Militaristic widower with garden gloves,
Armed with broom shuffling bristles,
Along concrete dance floor,
In windless afternoon hour,
Pushes leaves into garden walls corner.
Elements settle into a landscape of perfect order.

Fresh wind blowing in from the evening sky,
Fresh bluster of uplifted leaves in freefall.
Delightful dance of unattached leaves resumes
In carefree circulation of freedom.

CHRISTOPHER TITMUSS
Fire Dance and Other Poems

DESCENT FROM TUSHITA HEAVEN

FESTIVAL DAY ~ TWENTY-SECOND DAY
OF THE NINTH LUNAR MONTH

... INFINITE AND IMMEASURABLE WAS THE DISCOURSE WHICH WENT ON CEASELESSLY FOR THREE MONTHS WITH THE VELOCITY OF A WATERFALL ...

MRS. RHYS DAVIDS (*ed.*), PE MAUNG TIN (*trans.*)
The Expositor

The fourth extraordinary day in the Buddhist year marks the occasion of the Buddha's descent from the realm of the heavenly gods, the Tushita heaven. The *Pali Commentaries*, drawing upon an ancient oral tradition, maintain that just prior to the retreat of the seventh annual rains, the Buddha ascended to the Tushita heaven and taught the Abhidharma to an assembly of gods from the ten thousand world systems. The chief recipient of this teaching was his mother, who had died seven days after giving birth and was reborn as a god. Because the Abhidharma had to be expounded from beginning to end to the same audience in a single session – which takes three months – it had to be taught in the god realms. Only the gods were capable of remaining in one posture for that length of time.

Each day, to sustain his body, the Buddha would descend to the human world to go on his alms round. After eating his meal and resting in a sandalwood forest, he would give a synopsis of the teaching to his disciple Sariputra. It is said that while the Buddha was sustaining himself in this way, he manifested another perfect Buddha to continue preaching the doctrine. The commentary states, "there was no difference between the Supreme Buddha and the created Buddha as regards their rays, voices, or words" *(The Expositor)*.

❁ THE ABHIDHARMA is Buddhist psychology dealing with the five "skandhas," or psycho-physical constituents: form, feeling, perception, concept, and consciousness. It deals not only with the structure of human psychology but also with its pattern of evolution and the pattern of the evolution of the world. So vast and comprehensive is the Abhidharma that, while contemplating it, the Buddha's body lit up.

In the fourth week after the Enlightenment, while the Blessed One was still dwelling in the vicinity of the Bodhi Tree ... he contemplated the seven books of the Abhidharma Pitaka ... When he began to contemplate the twenty-four universal conditional relations of root, object and so on, his omniscience certainly found its opportunity therein … Rays of six colors – indigo, golden, red, white, tawny, and dazzling – issued from the teacher's body, as he was contemplating the subtle and abstruse dhamma by his omniscience which had found such opportunity.

MAHATHERA NARADA (*trans. and ed.*)
A Comprehensive Manual of Abhidharma

✳ THE ABHIDHARMA analyzes the world scientifically, in terms of "dharmas," successsions of impersonal momentary events. Here is a contemporary teaching of the "skandha" or psycho-physical constituent of feeling, based on the Abhidharma system.

Feeling consists of the pleasurable and the painful … This development of relating to things in terms of positive or negative value is a result of the basic pattern of ego established by form, the first skandha …These dualistic criteria … are the starting point for feeling.

…When we talk about feeling, we usually think in terms of feeling toward someone else: you fall in love with someone, you are angry with someone. In that imagery the other person is all-important and you are insignificant. On the other hand: you feel slighted or you want to be loved. In that case you are all-important and the others are insignificant. Feeling plays that introvert-extrovert game of making itself important by reflecting off "other." But in reality all that is very remote. Nobody is actually involved but yourself. You are alone and are creating the whole game by yourself.

… Feeling involves the pretense that you are involved with somebody; but actually you are just beating your own head against a wall …

That is why the buddhadharma is an atheistic teaching … Studying … feeling can be extremely important in helping us to realize that the whole journey is made alone, independent of anybody else.

…The mind aspect of it provides tremendous resources for this delusive process, inexhaustible sources of dreaming and imagining … this kind of feeling on the mind level – in ordinary situations, in the drug experience, in meditation – provides all kinds of occasions for dwelling on spiritual materialism. Spiritual materialism means relating to experiences in terms of their possible benefit to ego … [It] tends to associate anything to do with spirituality with a dream world or heaven, with something that has nothing to do with the body situation, with something that altogether bypasses the kitchen sink.

CHOGYAM TRUNGPA
Glimpses of Abhidharma

ANNIVERSARY OF MASTER DOGEN ZENJI

FIRST DAY OF SEPTEMBER

GREAT MASTER DOGEN (1200–1253) IS THE FOUNDER OF SOTO ZEN,
DISTINGUISHED FROM RINZAI ZEN BY A MORE RELAXED APPROACH.
HIS MOST INFLUENTIAL WRITING IS THE *SHOBOGENZO*.

Zen master Dogen came from an aristocratic background but lost his parents at an early age, a traumatic experience that impressed upon him the transitoriness of human existence. He became a monk at the age of thirteen, studied Buddhism in China, and was intellectually outstanding. At the tender age of twenty-seven, his enlightenment was recognized by his master. He returned to Japan to propagate Soto Zen, the Japanese form of one of the two major surviving branches of Chinese Ch'an. Soto Zen is distinguished from Rinzai Zen by a softer attitude summed up in the maxim: "Rinzai is for the general, Soto for the farmer." He established a temple in a remote corner of Japan in order to emphasize the importance of sitting meditation over the worldly pursuit of name and fame. He died at the age of fifty-two.

DOGEN LEFT behind some very influential writings, notably the *Shobogenzo (The Eye and Treasury of the True Dharma)*, from which this famous teaching is taken.

> To study the Buddha way is to study the self,
> To study the self is to forget the self.
> To forget the self is to be enlightened by the ten
>   thousand dharmas.
> To be enlightened by the ten thousand dharmas is to
>   free one's body and mind and those of others.
> No trace of enlightenment remains, and this traceless
>   enlightenment is continued forever.
>
> DOGEN ZENJI, HAKUYU TAIZAN *(commentator)*
> *The Way of Everyday Life*

❉ DOGEN ALSO wrote about the use of words and concepts to explain indescribable illumination.

They passed aeons living alone in the mountains and forests, only then did they unite with the Way and use mountains and rivers for words, raise the wind and rain for a tongue, and explain the great void.

ALLAN HUNT BADINER (*ed.*)
Shobogenzo, *Dharma Gaia*

❦

❉ BUDDHIST MASTERS teach profound insight meditation to enable one to see the interpenetration of phenomena and mind, and unravel the mystery of existence. This engenders wisdom so that we reach a genuine clear, nonconceptual, knowledge of birthlessness and deathlessness.

It is fallacious to think that you simply move from birth to death. Birth from the Buddhist point of view is a temporary point between the preceding and the succeeding; hence it can be called birthlessness. The same holds for death and deathlessness. In life there is nothing more than life, in death nothing more than death: we are being born and are dying at every moment.

DOGEN ZENJI,
PHILIP KAPLEAU (*ed.*)
The Wheel of Life and Death

ANNIVERSARY OF BODHIDHARMA

EIGHTH DAY OF SEPTEMBER

BODHIDHARMA IS REVERED AS THE SUCCESSOR OF A MIND-TO-MIND TRANSMISSION ORIGINATING WITH THE BUDDHA THROUGH HIS DISCIPLE MAHAKASHYAPA. THE ANNIVERSARY OF THE FIRST PATRIARCH OF ZEN IS CELEBRATED ON 8 SEPTEMBER.

The Indian Buddhist scholar Bodhidharma dropped in on the Chinese emperor in A.D. 520, one thousand years after the birth of the Buddha. Asked to define the fundamental principle of Buddhism, he replied, "Vast Emptiness," and departed to meditate facing a rock wall for nine years. When he came out of retreat, he offered the following verse, which is the essence of Zen.

> *A special transmission outside the scriptures;*
> *No dependence on words and letters;*
> *Direct pointing to the soul of man;*
> *Seeing into one's own nature and attainment of*
> *Buddhahood.*
>
> ANDREW POWELL
> *Living Buddhism*

❋ BODHIDHARMA TAUGHT by quoting the Buddha's essential message conveyed in the *Lankavatara Sutra*, which states:

> *"Mind is the source [of enlightenment], its doctrine, no fixed doctrine at all."* All who seek the Dharma should realize there is nothing fixed to seek for. Outside of mind there is no other Buddha, outside of Buddha there is no other mind.
>
> LU KUAN YU (*trans.*)
> Ma Tsu's Talks of Instruction
> *Ch'an and Zen Teachings*

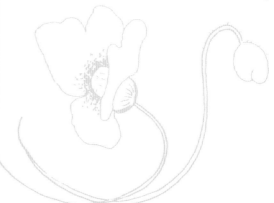

❁ BODHIDHARMA WAS the successor of a mind-to-mind transmission lineage originating in a particular moment when the Buddha, for no apparent reason, suddenly held up a flower and showed it to his assembly of disciples.

He did not say anything for quite a long time. The audience was perfectly silent. Everyone seemed to be thinking hard, trying to see the meaning behind the Buddha's gesture. Then, suddenly, the Buddha smiled. He smiled because someone in the audience smiled at him and at the flower. The name of that monk was Mahakashyapa … The Buddha smiled back and said, "I have a treasure of insight and I have transmitted it to Mahakashyapa." … To me the meaning is quite simple. When someone holds up a flower and shows it to you, he wants you to see it. If you keep thinking, you miss the flower. The person who was not thinking, who was just himself, was able to encounter the flower in depth, and he smiled.

THICH NHAT HANH
Peace Is Every Step

ANNIVERSARY OF
SUNLUN SAYADAW

OCTOBER

THE BURMESE TEACHER, SUNLUN SAYADAW (1878–1952),

THOUGH BARELY LITERATE, ATTAINED ARAHATSHIP

IN OCTOBER, 1920.

Sunlun Sayadaw was born at the cave monasteries of Sunlun Village in Burma. He went to the local monastery school but discontinued his education at fifteen. He married and became a farmer. Disturbed by intimations of his imminent death, he began to practice insight meditation. After practicing intensely for a while he began to be aware of touch and sensation in everything he did. Soon he began to see colored lights and geometrical patterns, the signs of intense practice. In mid-1920 he rapidly gained the three successive stages of liberation. He practiced diligently in the nearby caves and attained arahatship – the final stage of liberation in the Theravadin tradition – in the month of October, 1920. The monks tested his achievement and, though he was barely literate, his answers were authenticated by scriptural texts. Many learned monks from all over the world came to study with him. It is said that one of his disciples also became enlightened.

Sunlun Sayadaw's method is characterized by rigorous mindfulness of breathing and direct perception of sensation, especially pain. Jack Kornfield writes, "In a short time ... one may experience the power of a calm, concentrated mind, which, when applied to the mind-body process, leads to clear insight, wisdom, and liberation" (*Living Buddhist Masters*).

There are two forms of the practice of mental culture [meditation]. These are known as Samatha, or concentration practice, and Vipassana, or insight practice. Samatha leads to calm and tranquillity, and Vipassana leads to intuitive knowledge of the true nature of phenomena and consequent liberation. Samatha is concerned with the universe as it is for us; Vipassana is concerned with the universe as it is in itself ... The objects of meditation which lead to Samatha are accordingly those objects which we have made for ourselves ... The stability of earth, the cohesion of water, the maturing of fire, the interception of air are qualities of the four elements which have been conceptualized by us to help us in grasping them ... whatever makes the universe for us leads to Samatha; ... There is nothing wrong in Samatha in itself ... But concentration is not insight. Therefore, he who would gather the fruits of concentration may practice concentration, but he who desires to gather the fruits of insight will have to practice insight.

From a talk by one of the chief disciples
of Sunlun Sayadaw in JACK KORNFIELD
Living Buddhist Masters

✸ MEDITATION HAS two aspects. The first one is tranquility, or calming the mind; the second is insight into the true nature of the mind. Calming the mind is a prerequisite to insight.

There is an anecdote about a monk training under Sunlun Sayadaw. The monk was meditating on corpses; as he was setting out to the cremation ground one day he met Sunlun Sayadaw, who said to him, "The breathing exercise is free of dangers." The monk continued to meditate on corpses. One evening when he returned to his cell he yelled in terror, for there lying on the threshold was a corpse. That corpse was the "acquired image" of his concentration practice.

PAVARANA DAY

RAINY SEASON MEDITATION RETREAT

FULL MOON IN OCTOBER

The rainy season, or monsoon, in India lasts for three months every year, during which time travel is difficult and illness is prevalent. So the Buddha initiated a Rainy-Season Retreat, beginning in July and ending in October. It is still observed by Buddhist monks in India, particularly those in the Theravadin tradition. Meditation retreats are considered essential in all traditions of Buddhism. The traditional Tibetan three-year retreat, which is structured around sixteen hours of meditation a day, is now practiced in many Western countries.

During the Buddha's time, monks and nuns went into the forests of India to practice meditation. In Tibet, mountain caves were used by yogis and yoginis. These days the tradition continues in remote areas of Tibet and the Himalayan Buddhist countries. Adapting to the different requirements of Western culture, retreats are now conducted in simple buildings in the remote countryside.

> In retreat with one place to sleep,
> Avoiding every laziness,
> Live in the forest all alone
> And all alone subdue yourself.
>
> Whoever triumphs over self
> Achieves a conquest greater than
> The conquerors who win
> A hundred thousand victories in war.
>
> GARETH SPARHAM (*trans.*)
> *The Tibetan Dhammapada*

MEDITATION PRACTICE requires diligence and perseverance to achieve a result. There is the famous story of Milarepa's last instructions to his spiritual heir, Gampopa. The enlightened master bent down, pulled up his ragged robe and displayed his bare buttocks, hardened with calluses after years of sitting in meditation on bare rock. His secret instruction was quite simple: just *do* it.

Apply yourself both now and in the next life.
Without effort, you cannot be prosperous.
Though the land be good,
You cannot have an abundant crop without
  cultivation.

NAGARJUNA AND SAKYA PANDITA
Elegant Sayings

TRANQUILITY

WINTER

DECEMBER ❖ JANUARY ❖ FEBRUARY

Tranquility is the end of the path, or the state of no path. It comes from letting go of all fixation, understanding the unborn, undying nature of phenomena. It's like space or the transparent nature of crystal. In fact, it is indescribable. As the Lankavatara Sutra *puts it,*

Things are not what they seem,
Nor are they otherwise.

In this sutra, the Buddha suddenly holds up a flower and looks at it. Of his disciples only one, Mahakashyapa, sees any importance in this gesture and he asks no questions and only smiles. This is known as the awakening of indescribable illumination. The beginning and the end are one. No path.

Remaining in awareness is the winter of the mind. Thoughts come and go without disturbing the state of meditation because the root of distraction – attachment and aversion – has been illuminated. "The heart of the wise man is tranquil," Chuang Tzu wrote.

> *It is the mirror of heaven and earth, the glass of everything. Emptiness, stillness, tranquility ... this is the level of heaven and earth. This is perfect Tao. Wise men find here their resting place.*
>
> JOSEPH GOLDSTEIN
> *The Experience of Insight*

The light of mind exposes the fiction of ego-clinging as surely as the sun at midday destroys shadow. The discovery is that there has never been a shadow from the beginning. Zen Master Ikkyu writes:

> *Rain, sleet, snow, ice –*
> *As such they may be different, but when melted,*
> *they're the same valley stream, water.*
>
> THOMAS CLEARY *(trans. and ed.)*
> *The Original Face,*
> *An Anthology of Rinzai Zen*

Tranquility and insight reveal the inherent nature of mind. Tranquility is not a comatose state of utter passivity, but the state of letting everything be itself. In that state of quiescence, of not having to feed an interpretation into phenomena, everything has its own thingness. It is as it is.

The Zen and Ch'an schools of Buddhism emphasize disciplined sitting meditation for long periods of time to achieve tranquility, from which insight into the nature mind, or satori, is born. As we have seen, Bodhidharma, the first patriarch of Zen, brought the wordless transmission of the Buddha's mind-to-mind teaching to China, from where it went to Japan. Transmission, in fact, is the living breath of the Buddha's dharma. There is no possibility of obtaining enlightenment without it, in any tradition.

It is the living quality of enlightened mind from guru to disciple in an unbroken chain from the time of the Buddha. Without the transmission of the unnameable, unthinkable, inexpressible state of the nature of mind, Buddhism would simply be a collection of interesting, possibly provocative theories.

Tranquility is the expression of both the beginning and the end of the path. It deepens in all the seasons of the year. It's the basis of awakening, blossoming, and fruition. As it deepens, it reveals the unchanging season, the nature of mind. To quote a Zen saying, "The deep broad sky is untroubled by the passing clouds" *(The Ring of the Way).*

MEDICINE BUDDHA DAY

EIGHTH DAY OF THE MONTH

HEALTH IS THE GREATEST OF GIFTS, CONTENTMENT THE BEST OF RICHES.

The Dhammapada

The healing powers of a Buddha are enormous. The body of an enlightened one is a container for the limitless expanse which is itself the essence of holiness. That holiness is the ultimate healing power, the source of health, contentment, peace, loving-kindness, bliss – all the attributes of radiant harmony and wholeness.

The color of the Medicine Buddha is the blue of lapis lazuli. This semi-precious stone was felt to have excellent healing properties.

※ SOME OF the most important teachings on spiritual healing were given by the Buddha to an assembly of humans, spirits, and celestial birds at the Blue Lotus Pond in the Monkey Grove at Vaisali. *The Lotus Sutra* describes the miraculous healing power of light, of gems, especially lapis lazuli, and of mantra.

At that time the Lord entered into the samadhi of universal light. All the pores of his body emitted multihued rays, illuminating the ... grove with the colors of the seven precious substances. The light rising above the grove became a jeweled canopy, and various [rare] phenomena ... appeared within the canopy.

... The Buddha's eyes radiated light which illumined the foreheads of the two bodhisattvas, King of Healing and Supreme Healer. Above their heads all the limitless buddhas ... dazzlingly manifested like a diamond mountain, and all [of them] ... also emitted light from their eyes, which ... illumined the foreheads of all the bodhisattvas [in the assembly] ... resembling a lapis lazuli mountain ... a jeweled lotus blossom arose in the ... pond. It was the color of a white gem, but ... a white so rare that there was nothing to which it can be compared.

Various ... buddhas were seated on the lotus blossom, their bodies subtle and sublime ... Each radiated light from his eyes which illumined ... the foreheads of all the bodhisattvas.

...With a subtle smile of radiant harmony, the Buddha exhaled through his mouth five-colored rays which completely illumined his full moon like face... there were ... changing manifestations of light from the features of the Buddha's face, which appeared a million times more glorious than his ordinary appearance.

RAOUL BIRNBAUM
The Healing Buddha

IN ANOTHER healing sutra, the Buddha tells his disciple, Manjushri, of the vows that the healing Buddha, "Lapis Lazuli Radiance," made when he first set out on the path.

I vow that when I attain ... complete enlightenment ... a radiant light will blaze forth from my body. It will brilliantly illumine ... boundless realms ...

I vow that when I attain enlightenment ... my body will be like lapis lazuli ... bright with penetrating and flawless purity ... My body will be an excellent and tranquil dwelling, adorned with [an aura] ... surpassing the sun and moon in its radiance. I will show the dawn to those beings ... concealed in darkness ...

I vow that when I attain enlightenment ... if there are sentient beings whose bodies are inferior, whose sense organs are impaired, who are ugly, stupid, deaf, blind, mute, bent and lame, hunchbacked, leprous, convulsive, insane ... when they hear my name shall obtain proper appearances and practical intelligence. All their senses will become perfect and they shall have neither sickness nor suffering.

RAOUL BIRNBAUM
The Healing Buddha

PADMASAMBHAVA DAY

TENTH DAY OF THE MONTH

THE FALLING SNOW IN THE YEAR'S END BLIZZARD
FOUGHT ME, THE COTTON-CLAD, HIGH ON SNOW MOUNTAIN ...
I CONQUERED THE RAGING WINDS — SUBDUING THEM TO SILENT REST.

GARMA C.C. CHANG (*trans.*)
The Hundred Thousand Songs of Milarepa

ॐ

Padmasambhava Day in the winter is an appropriate time to pay homage to the Tantric Buddha's last activity on this planet. Padmasambhava, unlike the Buddha, never died. Because he hadn't entered the world through the portal of a womb, he was not subject to the natural law of birth and death. The parting scene is heroic, wondrous, and dramatic. When we look at Padmasambhava's predictions regarding the future of this planet — environmental and spiritual — we can have confidence in the omniscience of the enlightened mind and the supernormal powers of the body that accompany it.

Padmasambhava's body is described as a supreme vajra body, not subject to the laws of dissolution and decay of the ordinary human form. The texts record a miraculous life stretching from about 460 B.C. to about A.D. 830. It is believed that Padmasambhava attained the siddhi of immortality at Maratika Cave in Nepal, where he meditated in union with his foremost Indian consort, Mandarava, on Amitayus, the Buddha of Long Life.

After fifty-five years of empowering Tibet by teaching the path, concealing treasures for the future, and meditating in remote caves, he departed on his magical horse for another realm.

Padmasambhava's compassion does not rise and fall;
... One need only ask, and Padmasambhava
  will appear before him.
I am never far from those with faith;
or even far from those without it,
though they do not see me ...

Thus in the future on the tenth day of the month,
Padmasambhava will appear on the sun's rays.
As the four seasons change, so shall I,
from peaceful to wrathful forms,
and I shall give my children the siddhis they desire ...

On the fifteenth day, I will come on moon rays,
with blessings and compassion shaking the world;
I will empty all the lower realms,
benefiting all beings with my perfect charismatic action.

On the eighth day, night and daybreak, dawn and dusk,
mounted on the magical horse Cang-shes,
I will wander the world giving aid
  and strength to beings.

... I will manifest without distinction
in peaceful and wrathful forms,
as fire, water, air, space, and rainbows –
my vibrations passing everywhere,
my many manifestations leading to bliss.

NAMKHAI NYINGPO. TÁRTHANG TULKU (*trans.*)
Mother of Knowledge

PART OF Padmasambhava's legacy for future generations are predictions concerning the cycles of expansion and decline of human civilization on this planet. These were pronounced to his disciples in eighth-century Tibet, written down, and concealed until the predesignated time for their revelation came.

... This world, impermanent like a city of illusion, will not last long but is subject to destruction and change. Good or bad, day or night are all alike, for the cycle of rise and fall is like spring, summer, autumn, and winter. Because of the force of outer ... conflicts of elements, many natural catastrophes will occur ... during the end of this decadent age, fire will fail and create imbalance of heat and cold; water will fail and transmute wet and dry; earth will fail and hurl, destroy or shake; wind will fail and cause undue wavering; space will fail and reveal many different colors ... Torrential rain will fall and transmute the surroundings ...

Years, months, seasons, sun, moon, planets, and stars will deviate. The earth will lose its fertility and the forests will dry up. The luster of the surroundings will wane and hurricanes of red dust will blow. Unclean and misty smoke will billow the sky ...

... Like the breaking of a pool, the teachings of Sakyamuni will gradually vanish and finally be enshrouded in darkness ... the disturbances caused by the elements will be beyond words.

NORMA LEVINE
Blessing Power of the Buddhas

FULL MOON DAY

FIFTEENTH DAY OF THE MONTH

THE "NON-MOVEMENT" OF THINGS...DOES NOT MEAN THAT MOVEMENT MUST BE ARRESTED IN ORDER TO FIND QUIESCENCE, BUT THAT QUIESCENCE MUST BE SOUGHT WITHIN MOVEMENT.

SENG CHAO, On the Immutability of Phenomena, *Han Tang Fu Hsueh Si Hsiang Lun Chih*

❦

The full moon in winter has the quality of light and quiescence. Light itself is the source of the cosmic order. Light is also the quality of the mind's natural radiance. Returning to the source in the silence that illuminates creation, the lotus blossoms, the dreamer awakens.

The luminosity of mind arises as a result of finding quiescence within movement, the still center of the turning world. Quiescence and movement are inseparable from the beginning. Abiding in this state, mind flows together with everything.

We tend to think of movement and nonmovement as two separate states. To understand their inseparability, while moving, rest within nonmovement; know that movement happens within nonmovement.

The cosmos is movement and not-movement.
Movement is born of not-movement.
The two give rise to each other.
The planet's revolution is born of the
Immobility of the skies.
The eternal skies are born of light.
Light.
Source of the cosmic order.

TAISEN DESHIMARU
The Ring of the Way

✻ THE NATURE of mind is without limitation, but it cannot be seen. To look into the mind to try to contain it or measure it is to miss the true nature altogether.

Greater than heaven and earth put together,
it fills every place but no trace of it is found.
He is absurd who strains to see into the mind
in order to measure the void and bind the winds.

JAIHIUN KIM (*comp. and trans.*)
Poems by Zen Masters

✾ "FAITH IN MIND" by the Third Patriarch of Ch'an, who died in A.D. 606, is famous for describing the Great Way. Making distinctions, judging positive and negative, is the mind's disease. "I think therefore I am" is the very stuff that clouds the luminous nature of the mind. Extinguish all views, and "what is" appears by itself. Here are some excerpts of ancient wisdom from this lengthy poem.

The Perfect Way is only difficult for those who pick and choose;
Do not like, do not dislike; all will then be clear.
Make a hairbreadth difference, and Heaven and Earth are set apart;
If you want the truth to stand clear before you, never be for or against.
The struggle between "for" and "against" is the mind's worst disease.
… Stop all movement in order to get rest, and rest itself will be restless;
… Stop talking, stop thinking, and there is nothing you will not understand.
Return to the Root and you will find the meaning;
Pursue the light and you will lose its source …
There is no need to seek Truth; only stop having views …
In its essence the Great Way is all-embracing;
It is as wrong to call it easy as to call it hard …
If the mind makes no distinctions, all dharmas become one …
Take your stand on this, and the rest will follow of its own accord;
To trust in the heart is the Not Two, the Not Two is to trust in the heart.
I have spoken, but in vain; for what can words tell
Of things that have no yesterday, tomorrow, or today?

EDWARD CONZE (*trans.*)
Buddhist Texts through the Ages

DAKINI DAY

TWENTY-FIFTH DAY OF THE MONTH

WOMAN IS ESSENTIALLY WISDOM.

SOURCE OF SPONTANEOUS GNOSIS AND ILLUSORY-BODY.

MILAREPA,
LAMA KUNGA, THARTSE RINGPOCHE AND BRIAN CUTILLO (*trans.*)
Drinking the Mountain Stream

The word for dakini in Tibetan is khadro, literally sky-goer or sky-walker, one who moves through space. The wisdom mind of the dakini moves without obstruction through all phenomena, performing the activities of the Buddha. So the dakini has the powers of unimpeded movement. She has the quality of flowing, of making solid things transparent. She dances in the space of stillness, illuminating deluded appearances.

✲ THIS POEM shows the illuminating and spacious qualities of feminine wisdom.

> *When I meditate in the cave*
> *rock becomes transparent.*
> *When I met the right consort*
> *my thought became transparent.*
>
> CHOGYAM TRUNGPA
> *Mudra*

Detail from Arearea
PAUL GAUGUIN,
1848–1903

✲ THE ETERNAL dance of male and female, whose essence are the seed syllables EH (feminine) and VAM (masculine), expresses the power of pure love, the creative energy of the universe. There is no question of possessing it. The dance is the expression of the primal spark that sets the universe in motion. When we are ready we can join the dance of love.

THE PERFECT LOVE POEM

There is a beautiful snow peaked mountain
With peaceful clouds wrapped round her shoulders.
The surrounding air is filled with love and peace.
What is going to be is what is,
That is love.

There is no fear of leaping into the immeasurable
*   space of love.*
Fall in love?
Or, are you in love?
Such questions cannot be answered,
Because in this peace of an all-pervading presence,
No one is in and no one is falling in.
No one is possessed by another.

. . . In the playground beautiful Dakinis are holding
*   hand drums, flutes and bells.*
Some of them, who are dancing, hold naked flames,
*   water, a nightingale,*
Or the whole globe of earth with the galaxies around it.
These Dakinis may perform their dance of death or birth
*   or sickness,*
I am still completely intoxicated, in love.
And with this love, I watch them circle.
This performance is all-pervading and universal,
So the sonorous sound of mantra is heard
As a beautiful song from the Dakinis ...

Then I knew I must surrender to the dance
And join the circle of Dakinis.
Like the confluence of two rivers,
EH the feminine and VAM the male,
Meeting in the circle of the dance.

Unexpectedly, as I opened myself to love, I was
*   acccepted.*
So there is no questioning, no hesitation,
I am completely immersed in the all-powerful, the joyous
*   Dakini mandala.*
And here I found unwavering conviction that love
*   is universal.*
Five chakras of one's body filled with love,
Love without question, love without possessions ...

So the clear, peaceful mountain air,
Gently blows the clouds,
A beautiful silk scarf wrapped round,
The Himalayas with their high snow peaks are dancing,
Joining my rhythm in the dance,
Joining with the stillness, the most dignified movement
*   of them all.*

CHOGYAM TRUNGPA
Mudra

PROTECTOR DAY

TWENTY-NINTH DAY OF THE MONTH

IF FEAR COMES FROM THE PROTECTOR, WHO WILL PROTECT FROM FEAR?

NAGARJUNA AND SAKYA PANDITA
Elegant Sayings

ॐ

Fear is a fundamental reflex of ego. There are two radically different attitudes to have in dealing with fear. One is to become defensive and protect oneself. The other is to look at it directly, open up completely, and become fearless. The first is the way of the coward; the other is that of the warrior. Wisdom Protectors are there to help one step out of the cowardly kind of fear and to serve the fearless warrior.

The element of space, the clarity of crystal, and the color of pure white set the tone for Protector Day in the winter.

The warrior ... is someone who is not afraid of space. The coward lives in constant terror of space. When the coward is alone in the forest and doesn't hear a sound ... he begins to bring up ... monsters and demons in his mind ... Cowardice is turning the unconditional into ... fear by inventing reference points, or conditions, of all kinds. But for the warrior, unconditionality doesn't have to be conditioned or limited. It does not have to be qualified as either positive or negative, but it can just be neutral – as it is.

... The challenge of warriorship is ... to step out of the cocoon ... into space, by being brave and at the same time gentle. You can expose your wounds and flesh, your sore points ...

... The way to rule the universe is to expose your heart, so that others can see your heart beating, see your red flesh, and see the blood pulsating through your veins and arteries ...

This is the fruition of the warriorship, the complete primordial realization of basic goodness. At that level, there is absolutely no doubt about basic goodness or, therefore, about yourself. When you expose your naked flesh to the universe can you say, "Should I put a second skin on? Am I too naked?" You can't. At that point there is no room for second thoughts. You have nothing to lose and nothing to gain. You simply expose your heart completely.

CHOGYAM TRUNGPA
Shambhala

Legends claim that one of the important Tibetan protectors, named Genyen Phying Karba, was originally taken to Tibet from Nalanda in India by the scholar-saint Atisha. He is believed to be an aspect of the compassionate Chenresig, guardian of the Land of Snow.

Protectors are not only fearsome and black, encircled by flames, but can also be transparent like crystal, and like this one, adorned with all the attributes of pacifying: a great white horse, a jeweled palace, and a meadow of medicinal herbs.

On [the center of] a beautiful mountain-meadow, adorned with … medicinal herbs and forests of various trees … rises a palace made of crystal, turquoise, and gold … In it is … an excellent horse — great and white like a tremendous … snow mountain — possessing the swiftness of a cloud, adorned with a saddle … made of jewels; on top of [him] resides [the Protector] … The color of his body is similar to that of a mountain crystal … In his right hand he holds a long lance of white crystal possessing a sharp point of gold … with a billowing flag of heavenly silk attached to it. With his left hand he holds the wish-granting gem … He wears a turban … a dress with broad sleeves made of … silk, and he sits in a proud posture.

RENE DE NEBESKY-WOJKOWITZ
Oracles and Demons of Tibet

NEW MOON DAY

THIRTIETH DAY OF THE MONTH

**SNOWFLAKES, THOUGH AT A GLANCE BEAUTIFUL AS
FLOWERS, VANISH WHEN TOUCHED BY THE HAND.**

THINLEY NORBU
Magic Dance

ॐ

The volume of words the Buddha uses, from the first turning of the wheel of dharma right up to his final message before he passed away, was for one purpose only: to prepare the ground for pointing out the nature of mind. When all the conditions are there for realization of the true nature, then any experience can trigger it. The ultimate nature can only be pointed to; it cannot be expressed in words or images. That's why the winter new moon is empty, like an echo, like a dream, like a mirage, like the sounds of silence.

❋ THE *LANKAVATARA SUTRA* is one of the last discourses of the Buddha, much studied especially in the Zen tradition. As in a great cosmic play, words are unmasked, stripped of conceptual clothes, and the naked truth revealed.

The truths of the emptiness, unbornness, no self-natureness, and the nonduality of all things … is … presented to meet the varied dispositions of all beings. But it is not the Truth itself. These teachings are only a finger pointing toward Noble Wisdom. They are like a mirage with its springs of water which the deer take to be real and chase after. So with the teachings in all the sutras … they are not the Truth itself, which can only be self-realized within one's deepest consciousness.

… Words are dependent upon letters but meaning is not: meaning is … unborn. The Tathagatas do not teach a Dharma that is dependent upon letters. Anyone who teaches a doctrine that is dependent upon letters and words is a mere prattler, because Truth is beyond letters, words, and books.

THE BUDDHA
Lankavatara Sutra, A Buddhist Bible

❁ FOR TWELVE years Naropa, the great scholar of Nalanda University, followed the "mind-blowing" advice of the ragged fisherman Tilopa, one of the great Indian mahasiddhas. During this time Naropa leaped off a building, jumped into a fire, was stoned nearly to death and beaten up four times, was bitten by leeches and frozen in a lake, and severed his limbs to offer to his guru. Each time Tilopa healed him and gave precious instructions that have survived and are known as the Six Yogas of Naropa. Finally, Naropa received these instructions pointing out the nature of mind.

Walk the hidden path of the Wish-Fulfilling Gem
Leading to the realm of the heavenly tree, the changeless.
Untie the tongue of mutes.
Stop the stream of samsara, of belief in an ego.
Recognize your very nature as a mother knows her child.

This is transcendent awareness cognizant in itself,
Beyond the path of speech, the object of no thought.
I, Tilopa, having nothing at which to point,
Know this as pointing in itself to itself.

Do not imagine, think, deliberate,
Meditate, act, but be at rest.
With an object do not be concerned,
Spirituality, self-existing, radiant,
In which there is no memory to upset you
Cannot be called a thing.

HERBERT GUENTHER (*trans.*)
The Life and Teaching of Naropa

MAGHA PUJA DAY

FESTIVAL DAY ~ FULL MOON IN FEBRUARY

**MORAL CONDUCT IS THE ... FOUNDATION
AND THE CHIEF CAUSE OF ALL GOOD THINGS.
IT IS THE BOUNDARY ... AND THE BRIGHTENING OF THE MIND.
THUS ONE SHOULD PURIFY MORAL CONDUCT.**

K.R. NORMAN (*trans.*)
The Elder's Verses: Theragatha and Therigatha

This day commemorates the time when the Buddha taught the foundation of moral conduct, or discipline, to a gathering of 1,250 disciples. The occasion was a full-moon-day feast that King Bimbisara of Magahda prepared for the Buddha and his community of monks. When they had all finished eating, the king requested the Buddha to teach the dharma. The Buddha taught the five precepts as the basis of happiness for the entire kingdom.

The first precept is do not kill. Observing this precept nourishes compassion … As we cherish our own lives, we should cherish the lives of all other beings … We should strive to avoid taking the lives of other species … If we nourish a heart of love, we can reduce suffering and create a happy life. If every citizen observes the precept not to kill, the kingdom will have peace. When people respect each other's lives, the country … will be safe from invasion …

The second precept is do not steal. No one has the right to take away the possessions that another has earned by his own labor … If the citizens observe this precept, social equality will flower and robbing and killing will quickly cease.

The third precept is avoid sexual misconduct. Sexual relations should only take place with your spouse. Observing this precept builds trust and happiness in the family …

The fourth precept is do not lie. Do not speak words that can create division and hatred … Words have the power to create trust and happiness, or they can create misunderstanding and hatred and even lead to murder and war.

The fifth precept is do not drink alcohol or use other intoxicants … Intoxicants rob the mind of clarity. When someone is intoxicated he can cause untold suffering to himself, his family, and others …

If you see to it that those under your charge understand and observe the five … principles of living in peace and harmony, the country of Magahda will thrive.

THICH NHAT HANH
Old Path, White Clouds

ANNIVERSARY OF JE TSONGKHAPA

TWENTY-FIFTH DAY OF THE TENTH LUNAR MONTH

TSONGKHAPA (1357–1419) WAS AN IMPORTANT MONASTIC REFORMER, FOUNDER OF THE GELUG SCHOOL OF TIBETAN BUDDHISM. THE LINEAGE OF THE DALAI LAMAS COMES FROM TSONGKHAPA'S DISCIPLES, THUS ESTABLISHING THE GELUGPA AS THE RULING SECT OF TIBET.

༄༅

The fourteenth-century master Je Tsongkhapa was the founder of the Gelug (literally, the virtuous) school of Tibetan Buddhism. He was identified as a manifestation of the bodhisattva of wisdom, Manjushri. Tsongkhapa founded Ganden, one of the great monastic universities of Tibet, and also established the great prayer festival of "Monlam Chenmo" in Lhasa just after the new year.

Tsongkhapa was a reformer, challenging what he believed were the dharmically incorrect views of some of the other Buddhist schools. He emphasized monasticism, intense study, particularly of the Indian masters of philosophy and logic, and developed the Lam Rim Chenmo, the graduated stages of the path to enlightenment. From Tsongkhapa's disciples came the lineage of the Dalai Lamas. Thereafter, the Gelug became the ruling sect of Tibet until the Chinese invasion.

Buddhists understand that the cause of all the suffering in the world is ignorance, not knowing our true nature. There is no such thing as original sin. The original face or nature is Buddha-nature, and that is the stainless seed of perfect Buddhahood.

> *Whatever faults there are in this world*
> *Their root is ignorance*
>
> JE TSONGKHAPA
> Praise of Dependent Relationship,
> *Joyful Path of Good Fortune*

✷ IN THE first turning of the wheel of dharma, the Buddha emphasized moral discipline as the starting point for attaining liberation from the cycle of existence. By Tsongkhapa's time some of the Buddhist schools had become somewhat relaxed. So, a reminder was necessary.

Moral discipline is water to cleanse the stains of faults,
A ray of moonlight to cool the scorching heat of delusions,
Splendor towering as a mountain in the midst of beings,
Force subjugating all without recourse to intimidation.

Knowing this, the holy ones, guarded as they would their own eyes
Their perfectly adopted discipline.
I, a yogi, practiced this way,
You who seek liberation, please do the same.

JE TSONGKHAPA, J. SAMUELS (*trans.*)
Condensed Exposition on the
Stages of the Path

ANNIVERSARY OF LONGCHENPA

EIGHTEENTH DAY OF THE TWELFTH LUNAR MONTH

LONGCHENPA (1308–1363) WAS A GREAT TIBETAN SCHOLAR, PHILOSOPHER, AND MYSTIC, WHO FREQUENTLY LIVED IN SECLUSION CLOSE TO NATURE.

Sarvavid with Eight Figures
19TH/20TH CENTURY

Longchen Rabjam (Doctor of Profound Meta-physics) was the greatest scholar, writer, philosopher, and mystic in the Nyingma school of Tibetan Buddhism since the time of Padmasambhava. From childhood Longchen possesssed the noble qualities of a bodhisattva: great intelligence, faith, and compassion. He became an extraordinarily learned yogi, wandering in various places, and studying with many celebrated scholars.

❋ LONGCHEN LIVED in harmony with nature, so his writings frequently show how nature is the foundation and support for realizing the inner nature of mind. Nature inspires enlightened nature.

Mind, listen to the virtues of the forests.
The precious trees, worthy objects to offer to the
  Buddhas,
Bend under the load of fruit that is growing splendidly.
Blossoming flowers and leaves emit sweet odors.
Fragrant scents fill the air …
The cool and clean ponds covered with lotuses
Radiate like smiling faces …
In forests emotions decline naturally.
There no one speaks unharmonious words …
In forests the peace of absorption grows …

In the forest, by the example of dead leaves
Come to realize that the body, youth, and senses
Change gradually and do not possess any true essence …
By the example of the separation of leaves and trees
Come to realize that friends, enemies, as well as one's
  own body,
… are bound to separate.
By the example of empty lotus ponds

Come to realize that various objects of desire, wealth,
  and prosperity
Are finally going to change, that there is no true essence
  in them,
… By the example of the change of days, months, and
  the four seasons,
Come to realize that the blossoming spring flowerlike body
Is subject to change as time passes, its youth fades away,
And the arrival of the lord of death is certain.
By the example of the fall of ripened fruit
Come to realize that … what is born will die.
By the example of the arising of reflections in ponds
Come to realize that various phenomena appear but have
  no true existence.
Having realized phenomena in that way …
Meditate on the mind of enlightenment.
Watch the ultimate peace, the intrinsic nature of the mind.

TULKU TONDUP
Buddha Mind

ANNIVERSARY OF ACHAAN CHAH

SIXTEENTH DAY OF JANUARY

THAI MASTER ACHAAN CHAH (1918–1992) WAS A FOREST MONK BEFORE ESTABLISHING THE MONASTERY OF WAT PAH BONG. IN 1979 HE VISITED ENGLAND WITH HIS DISCIPLE ACHAAN SUMEDHO AND FOUNDED CHITHURST HOUSE, A BUDDHIST SEMINARY IN THE HEART OF RURAL ENGLAND.

Achaan Chah was born in Thailand to a prosperous family and was well educated in the monastic tradition. It left him dissatisfied, however, for he realized when his father died that he was no closer to eradicating suffering. So at the age of twenty-eight, he set out to seek instruction in the practice of Buddhism – on foot, with no more than a begging bowl and a set of robes. Influenced by the renowned meditation master Ajahn Mun, he then became a forest monk for seven years, practicing meditation in the jungle. In 1954, together with some other forest monks, he founded the monastery of Wat Pah Bong. In 1977, at the invitation of the English Sangha Trust, Achaan Chah arrived in Britain with his disciple

Achaan Sumedho, an American ex-serviceman. They founded a Buddhist seminary, Chithurst House, which trains monks in a totally orthodox tradition. It has the distinction of being the first Buddhist community to be run entirely by Western monks and nuns. Achaan Chah's warm-hearted, Zen-like style has been such an inspiration to Westerners that about one hundred monasteries have sprung up worldwide. He died in 1992 after ten years of a paralyzing illness.

✳ ACHAAN CHAH'S teachings are as natural and clear as a still forest pool. They do not need any commentary.

Each person has his own natural pace. Some of you will die at fifty, some at age sixty-five, and some at age ninety. So too your practice will not be identical. Don't think or worry about this. Try to be mindful, and let things take their natural course. Then your mind will become still in any surroundings, like a clear forest pool. All kinds of wonderful, rare animals will come to drink at the pool, and you will clearly see the nature of all things. You will see many strange and wonderful things come and go, but you will be still. This is the happiness of the Buddha.

ACHAAN CHAH,
JACK KORNFIELD AND PAUL BREITER (*comp. and ed.*)
A Still Forest Pool

The Buddha told his disciple Ananda to see impermanence, to see death with every breath. We must know death; we must die in order to live. What does this mean? To die is to come to the end of all our doubts, all our questions, and just be here with the present reality. You can never die tomorrow, you must die now. Can you do it?

ACHAAN CHAH,
JACK KORNFIELD AND PAUL BREITER (*comp. and ed.*)
A Still Forest Pool

ANNIVERSARY
OF COL. HENRY S. OLCOTT
SEVENTEENTH DAY OF FEBRUARY

COL. HENRY S. OLCOTT (1832–1907) WAS THE COFOUNDER AND PRESIDENT OF THE THEOSOPHICAL SOCIETY AND WAS AMONG THE FIRST WESTERNERS TO BECOME A BUDDHIST. HE WAS A PASSIONATE REFORMER WHO DEVOTED HIS LIFE TO THE RENAISSANCE OF BUDDHIST CULTURE IN SOUTHEAST ASIA.

Col. Henry Steel Olcott, cofounder and president of the Theosophical Society, was an American who devoted his life to the renaissance of Buddhist culture and religion in Southeast Asia. So greatly is his contribution honored in Sri Lanka (formerly Ceylon) that February 17 is celebrated as Olcott Day.

Olcott became interested in Buddhism around the same time as he began to study the esoteric traditions of the East. When he learned of British suppression of Buddhism in Ceylon, he decided to go to Ceylon and set things right. Upon arriving on the island, he immediately took refuge in the Buddha in a great public ceremony, thereby becoming officially Buddhist. He was remarkably zealous, unlike most Buddhists and, accompanied by other Theosophists, he moved slowly through the villages lecturing to many thousands in the open air, stirring them to fight for the rights of Buddhists.

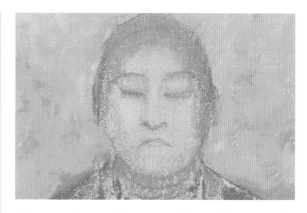

On a subsequent visit to Ceylon, Olcott, the "great white Buddhist," as he was dubbed, spent eight months traveling up and down the country by paddy boat and bullock cart collecting money for an education fund. Having found the Sinhalese to be shockingly ignorant of Buddhism, he spent his spare time writing a Buddhist catechism, an elementary handbook along the lines of those used by Christian sects. The book became a bestseller, went through more than forty printings, and was translated into more than twenty languages. As a result of Olcott's tireless efforts, the Sinhalese were given back their religious freedom and Wesak was declared a public holiday.

EPILOGUE

Do not forget that the earth is the refining furnace of the Ego, that the limitations of the physical, the inequalities of evolution and, in consequence, the impossibility of the majority of people realizing, even for a moment, their unity with the Universal Self, is the reason for so much sorrow ... No matter if your brother revile you, rise above the seeming: no matter if you are thrown down by seeming injustice; it can only be for a day: there are Powers that adjust the Karma of the individual to himself, so do not question Their Wisdom in these things, but remember the Law is unerringly true, just. Study well your motives, if they are right you need not have one moment's anxiety about your work, or the troubles coming to you: for remember all this inharmony is the result of ignorance, therefore do not allow yourself to be affected by it, otherwise you deliberately retard your advancement ... It is only through suffering that we can attain perfection, so ... be comforted; ... be courageous! Know that at such times your strength is being tested, and if you hold fast to your ideals, and are true to your own Higher Nature you are not alone, but sheltered by the Divine arms of Truth that will bring you all in good time to the joy and peace that passeth all understanding.

H.S. OLCOTT
Noble Theosophists Speak to Theosophists and to the World

The true men of old were not afraid when they stood alone in their views ... The true men of old slept without dreams, woke without worries. Their food was plain, they breathed deep ... The true men of old knew no lust for life, no dread of death. Their entrance was without gladness, their exit ... without resistance. Easy come, easy go. They did not forget where from, not ask where to. Nor drive grimly forward fighting their way through life. They took life as it came, gladly; took death as it came, without care; and went away, yonder ... These are the ones we call true men. Minds free, thoughts gone, brows clear, faces serene. Were they cool? Only cool as autumn. Were they hot? No hotter than spring. All that came of them came quiet, like the four seasons.

JOSEPH GOLDSTEIN
The Experience of Insight

GLOSSARY

ARHAT: *the highest stage of enlightenment in the Hinayana tradition. According to the Mahayana, however, it is not complete enlightenment, because it lacks the altruistic aspiration to benefit all beings.*

BODHISATTVA: *literally, one with the mind of enlightenment. One on the path to Buddhahood is a bodhisattva. In general, a bodhisattva works actively in the world for the benefit of all sentient beings.*

BUDDHA: *literally, "awakened," an enlightened one who is a perfected bodhisattva. The Buddha of our era is Sakyamuni, who lived in India 2500 years ago. There have been three Buddhas previous to Sakyamuni; and there are one thousand in this era, which is therefore known as the Fortunate Era.*

CHAKRAS: *the six nerve centers of the subtle body, situated along the spinal column from which psychic energy flows.*

CHENRESIG: *deity of compassion; the "patron saint" of Tibet. Sometimes called Avalokiteshvara.*

DAKINI: *female embodiment of a Buddha, demonstrating highest wisdom in a female form. There are five different classes of dakini, but only the Yeshes Khandro, the wisdom dakini, is enlightened.*

DHARMA: *phenomenon; also the truth of the Buddha's teachings, the Buddhist path.*

DHARMAPALA: *dharma protector, or wisdom protector of the dharma.*

EMANATION: *a projection; Buddhas, for example, can emanate innumerable forms.*

GNOSIS: *the state of knowing in itself, without an object; spiritual wisdom.*

KARMA: *literally, action. The natural law of cause and effect. Reaping what one sows. The purpose of the Buddhist path is to purify negative karmas and accumulate positive ones.*

KARMAPA: *known as the Black Hat Lama of Tibet and head of the Karma kamtsang branch of the Karma Kagyud sect of Tibetan Buddhism.*

KOAN: *a riddle designed to break through the rational, intellectual limitations of the mind and achieve awareness of unconditioned reality.*

MAHASIDDHA: *literally one of great power; refers to an accomplished yogi who can show miraculous powers, who has penetrated the illusion of appearance and can demonstrate its essential emptiness.*

MANDALA: *literally place, or center and surrounding, of any shape or size. A sacred mandala would be one with a deity at the center surrounded by a retinue or assembly placed in a significant formation from the center outwards to the perimeter.*

MANTRA: *sacred sounds, usually the essence of a deity; used to help concentrate the mind and arouse devotion.*

MARA: *temptations coming from one's own mind but seen dualistically as external forces.*

MARPA: *the great Tibetan translator (1012–1097) who went to India and received Tantric teachings and transmission from the Indian mahasiddha Naropa; guru of the great yogi Milarepa.*

MILAREPA: *Tibet's great yogi (1052–1135), disciple of Marpa; spent his life in remote caves and demonstrated miraculous powers.*

MUDRA: *gesture symbolizing particular spiritual attributes or steps toward perfection.*

NAGA: *powerful, long-living beings usually residing in water, often appearing as dragons or serpents; entrusted by the Buddha as guardians of the scriptures (The Prajnaparamita) and sacred objects. Their function is often to protect precious dharma teachings and objects.*

NAROPA: *an Indian mahasiddha (1016–1100), the disciple of Tilopa. Renowned for his scholarship, he became Abbot of Nalanda University before meeting Tilopa, who put him through twelve years of training with twelve tests that resulted finally in his enlightenment.*

PANDITA: *a learned teacher or scholar, generally of Indian origin.*

PARINIRVANA: *the death of Buddha – his passing into nirvana.*

PRAJNAPARAMITA: *literally, "highest wisdom." The Buddha delivered a discourse on Prajnaparamita at Vulture's Peak in India, the essence of which is that form is emptiness and emptiness no other than form. These teachings were concealed in the Naga Kingdom and revealed later by Nagarjuna.*

REALIZATION: *refers to all the stages of spiritual growth, from certainty of death to becoming a Buddha. Ultimate realization is enlightenment. From this point there is nothing further to develop.*

SAMADHI: *the state of meditative or concentrative absorption.*

SAMSARA: *the endless cycle of birth, old age, sickness, and death based on ignorance – on the mistaken notion of "I" and other, and the duality created by ego-clinging.*

SATORI: *indescribable enlightenment, often occurring suddenly.*

SEED SYLLABLE: *the alphabetical representation of the yidam, or Tantric deity.*

SIDDHI: *spiritual powers or miracles attained after long periods of meditative concentration; or at an enlightened level, occurring spontaneously with the fruition of wisdom – seeing the emptiness of all phenomena.*

SIKKIM: *one of the major hidden lands of Padmasambhava, bordering Bhutan, India, and Nepal. Until the mid-1970s, when it was forcibly annexed by India, it was an independent Buddhist kingdom with a lineage of Chogyals, known as spiritual kings.*

STUPA: *the Tibetan word chuten (stupa) means object of offering; it contains the relics of the Buddha, so devotees circumambulate it and make offerings to it. It may be dome-shaped or like a tower, with many stages or levels. It represents the body, speech, and mind of the Buddha in general; but if divided into three categories, then texts represent speech, images represent body, and the stupa represents the mind of the Buddha.*

SUTRA: *dialogue/discourse of the Buddha*

TANTRA: *literally, continuity or continuum. A Buddhist tradition of yogic practice frequently using ritual and mantra, based on texts called Tantras. Tantric yoga uses the raw energy of the emotions to transform into wisdom. In Tantric iconography the female is wisdom and the male, compassion. Their union is necessary for enlightenment.*

TATHAGATA: *title of Buddha – one who has achieved full realization.*

TERTONS: *the incarnations of the twenty-five special disciples of Padmasambhava whose destiny is to reveal particular sacred treasure and texts that were concealed by Padmasambhava to help beings in the future.*

TILOPA: *an Indian mahasiddha (988–1069) who received direct transmission of the teachings of Mahamudra from the primordial Buddha Vajradhara.*

VAJRA: *symbolic ritual object with five or nine points at each end, symbolizing wrathful skillful means for cutting through ego. It also refers to the male part.*

WESAK: *festival of the triple event of the Buddha's birth, enlightenment, and parinirvana in the Theravadin tradition, celebrated on the full moon of May.*

ZEN: *a straight pointing to the highest truth. Zen wisdom is poetic, imagistic, simple, profound, and nonintellectual.*

BIBLIOGRAPHY

Ashvaghosha, *Buddhacarita: Acts of the Buddha*, Motilal Banarsidass, New Delhi, 1984.

Allan Hunt Badiner, ed., *Dharma Gaia*, Parallax Press, Berkeley, Ca., 1990.

Stephen Batchelor, trans., Shantideva: *A Guide to the Bodhisattva's Way of Life*, Library of Tibetan Works and Archives, Dharamsala, India, 1979.

Raoul Birnbaum, *The Healing Buddha*, Shambhala Publications, Boston, Mass., 1979, 1989.

Ernest M. Bowden, compiler, *The Imitation of Buddha*, Methuen and Co., 1891.

Ajahn Buddhadasa, *Heartwood of the Bodhi Tree*, Wisdom Publications, Boston, Mass., 1994.

Garma C.C. Chang, trans., *The Hundred Thousand Songs of Milarepa*, Shambhala Publications, Boston, Mass., 1977.

Seng Chao, "On the Immutability of Phenomena", part 1, *Han Tang Fu Hsueh Si Hsiang Lun Chih*, Beijing, 1974.

Thomas Cleary, trans. and ed., *The Original Face, An Anthology of Rinzai Zen*, Grove Press, NY, 1978.

Edward Conze, trans. and ed., *Buddhist Texts through the Ages*, Bruno Cassirer, Oxford, 1954.

Edward Conze, trans. and ed., *Buddhist Scriptures*, Penguin Classics, Harmondsworth, Middlesex, 1959.

Tenzin Gyatso, The Fourteenth Dalai Lama, ed. by Daniel Goleman & Robert Thurman, *Mind Science, an East-West Dialogue*, Wisdom Publications, Boston, Mass., 1991.

Tenzin Gyatso, The Fourteenth Dalai Lama, commentary, *Generous Wisdom*, The Jatamakala, Library of Tibetan Works and Archives, Dharamsala, India, 1993.

Wm. Theodore de Bary, ed., *Sources of Japanese Tradition*, Columbia University Press, NY, 1958.

Taisen Deshimaru, *The Ring of the Way*, Testament of a Zen Master, E.P. Dutton, NY, 1983.

K. Sri Dhammananda, trans., *The Dhammapada*, Sasana Abhiwurdhi Wardhere Society, Kuala Lumpur, Malaysia, 1988.

Kenneth Douglas and Gwendolyn Bays, English trans., *The Life and Liberation of Padmasambhava*, Dharma Publishing, Berkeley, Ca., 1978.

Keith Dowman, trans., *Masters of Enchantment*, Inner Traditions Intl., Rochester, Vt., 1988.

L. Freer, ed., *Samyutta Nikaya*, Pali Text Society, Abingdon, 1884–89.

Morgan Gibson and Hiroshi Murakami, trans., *Tantric Poetry of Kukai*, White Pine Press, NY, 1982.

Dwight Goddard, ed., *A Buddhist Bible*, E.P. Dutton, 1938, reprinted Beacon Press, 1994.

Joseph Goldstein, *The Experience of Insight*, Unity Press, Santa Cruz, Ca., 1987.

Herbert Guenther, trans., *The Life and Teaching of Naropa*, Oxford University Press, Oxford, 1963.

Panchen Losang Chokyi Gyaltsan, trans., Geshe Kelsang Gyatso, *Offering to the Spiritual Guide*, Tharpa Publications, 1992.

Thich Nhat Hanh, *The Sun My Heart*, Parallax Press, Berkeley, Ca., 1988.

Thich Nhat Hanh, *Peace Is Every Step*, Bantam Books, NY, 1991.

Thich Nhat Hanh, *Old Path, White Clouds*, Parallax Press, 1991; Rider, London, 1992.

Shoda Harada, *Morning Dewdrops of the Mind*, North Atlantic Books, Berkeley, Ca., 1993.

Lex Hixon, *Mother of the Buddhas*, The Theosophical Publishing House, Wheaton., Ill., 1993.

John D. Ireland, trans., *The Udana*, Buddhist Publication Society, Sri Lanka, 1994.

Philip Kapleau, ed., *The Wheel of Life and Death*, Bantam Books, NY, 1989.

Jaihiun Kim, compiler and trans., *Poems by Zen Masters*, Hanshin Publishing Co., Seoul, Korea, 1988.

Jack Kornfield and Paul Breiter, compiler and ed., *A Still Forest Pool, The Insight Meditation of Achaan Chah*, The Theosophical Publishing House, Wheaton, Ill., 1985.

Jack Kornfield, *Living Buddhist Masters*, Buddhist Publication Society, Sri Lanka, 1988.

Jack Kornfield, *A Path with Heart*, Bantam Books, NY, 1993; Rider, London, 1995.

Lama Kunga, Thartse Rinpoche and Brian Cutillo, trans., *Drinking the Mountain Stream*, Wisdom Publications, Boston, Mass., 1995.

Norma Levine, *Blessing Power of the Buddhas*, Element Books, Shaftesbury, Dorset, 1993.

Longchenpa, *A Visionary Journey*, trans. and annotated by Herbert Guenther, Shambhala Publications, Boston, Mass., 1989.

Juan Mascaro, trans., *The Dhammapada*, Penguin Books, NY, 1973.

Glenn H. Mullin, trans., *Selected Works of the Dalai Lama VII: Songs of Spiritual Change*, Snow Lion Publications, Ithaca, NY, 1985.

Howard Murphet, *Yankee Beacon of Buddhist Light*, The Theosophical Publishing House, Wheaton, Ill., 1988.

Bhikku Nanamoli, *The Life of the Buddha*, Buddhist Publication Society, Sri Lanka, 1972.

Bhikku Nanamoli, trans., *The Middle Length Discourses of the Buddha*, Wisdom Publications,

Boston, Mass., 1995.

Mahathera Narada, trans. and ed., *A Comprehensive Manual of Abhidhamma*, Buddhist Publication Society, Sri Lanka.

Nagarjuna and Sakya Pandita, *Elegant Sayings*, Dharma Publishing, Emeryville, Ca., 1977.

Nebesky-Wojkowitz, *Oracles and Demons of Tibet*, Tiwari's Pilgrims Book House, Kathmandu, Nepal, 1993.

Thinley Norbu, *Magic Dance*, Jewel Publishing House, NY, 1981.

Thinley Norbu, *White Sail*, Shambhala Publications, Boston, Mass., 1992.

Louis Nordstrom, ed., *Namu Dai Bosa*, Theater Arts Books, NY, 1976.

K.R. Norman, trans., *The Elder's Verses: Theragatha and Therigatha*, vol. 1, Luzac, London, 1969.

Namkhai Nyingpo, trans., Tarthang Tulku, *Mother of Knowledge*, Dharma Publishing, Berkeley, Ca., 1983.

Henry S. Olcott, *The Buddhist Catechism*, The Theosophical Publishing House, Wheaton Ill., 1970.

Henry S. Olcott, *Noble Theosophists Speak to Theosophists and to the World*, The Theosophical Publishing House, Adyar, India.

Andrew Powell, *Living Buddhism*, British Museum Publications, London, 1989.

A.F. Price and Wong Mou-Lam, trans., *The Diamond Sutra and Sutra of Hui Neng*, Shambhala Publications, Boston, Mass., 1969.

Paul Reps, compiler, *Zen Flesh, Zen Bones*, Penguin Books, NY, 1971.

Mrs. Rhys Davids, ed., Pe Maung Tin, trans., *The Expositor*, Pali Text Society, London, 1976.

Saddhatissa, trans., *The Sutta Nipata*, Curzon Press, Richmond, Surrey, 1985.

Miranda Shaw, *Passionate Enlightenment*, Princeton University Press, Princeton, NJ, 1994.

Mu Soeng, *Thousand Peaks*, Parallax Press, Berkeley, Ca., 1987.

John Snelling, *The Buddhist Handbook*, Rider, London, 1987.

Gareth Sparham, trans., *The Tibetan Dhammapada*, Mahayana Publications, New Delhi, India, 1983.

John Stevens, trans., *One Robe One Bowl*, Weatherhill, NY, 1977.

D.T. Suzuki, trans, *Lankavatara Sutra*, Routledge and Kegan Paul, London, 1973.

Shunryu Suzuki, *Zen Mind, Beginner's Mind*, Weatherhill, NY, 1970.

Taisho Shinshu Daizokyo Kyokai, Tokyo, 1924–1935, vol xviii.

Hakuyu Taizan, commentator, *The Way of Everyday Life*, Zen Master Dogen's Genjokoan, MacZumi Center Publications, Los Angeles, Ca., 1978.

Tibetan Tripataka, Peking ed., 1763–95, reprinted Otani University, Kyoto, 1957.

Christopher Titmuss, *Fire Dance and Other Poems*, Insight Books, Devon, 1992.

Tulku Tondup, *Buddha Mind*, Snow Lion Publications, Ithaca, NY, 1989.

Yeshe Tsogyal, trans., Eric Pema Kunsang, *The Lotus-Born*, Shambhala Publications, Boston, Mass., 1993.

Je Tsongkhapa, "Praise of Dependent Relationship", *Joyful Path of Good Fortune*, trans. Geshe Kelsang Gyatso, Tharpa Publications, 1990.

Je Tsongkhapa, *Condensed Exposition on the Stages of the Path*, trans. J. Samuels, unpublished text.

Chogyam Trungpa, *Mudra*, Shambhala Publications, Boston, Mass., 1972.

Chogyam Trungpa, *The Myth of Freedom*, Shambhala Publications, Boston, Mass., 1987.

Chogyam Trungpa, *Glimpses of Abhidharma*, Prajna Press, Boulder, Co., 1978.

Chogyam Trungpa and Nalanda Translation Committee, *The Rain of Wisdom*, Shambhala Publications, Boston, Mass., 1980.

Chogyam Trungpa, *Shambhala, The Sacred Path of the Warrior*, Shambhala Publications, Boston, Mass., 1984.

Chogyam Trungpa, *Crazy Wisdom*, Shambhala Publications, Boston, Mass., 1991.

Chogyam Trungpa, *The Heart of the Buddha*, Shambhala Publications, Boston, Mass., 1991.

Tarthang Tulku, *Crystal Mirror*, vol. V and series I–III "Footsteps on the Diamond Path," Dharma Publishing, Emeryville Ca., 1977.

Uisang, "Ocean Seal of Huayen Buddhism" in Steve Odin, *Process Metaphysics and Hua Yen Buddhism*, State University of New York Press, NY, 1982.

Geshe Wangyal, quoted in *The Jewelled Staircase*, Snow Lion Publications, Ithaca, NY, 1986.

Martin Wilson, *In Praise of Tara*, Wisdom Publications, Boston, Mass., 1986.

Lu Kuan Yu (Charles Luk), trans., *Ch'an and Zen Teaching*, Rider, London, 1960.

Lu Kuan Yu (Charles Luk), trans., *The Vimalakirti Nirdesa Sutra*, Shambhala Publications, Boston, Mass., 1972.

Lu Kuan Yu (Charles Luk), trans., *The Transmission of Mind*, Rider, London, 1974.

ACKNOWLEDGEMENTS

The author and publishers are grateful to the following for permission to reproduce copyright material:

Bantam Books: from *Peace Is Every Step* by Thich Nhat Hanh, copyright 1991 by Thich Nhat Hanh (pp.19, 27, 55, 87); *A Path With Heart* by Jack Kornfield. Copyright 1993 by Jack Kornfield (p.33); *The Wheel of Life and Death* by P. Kapleau. Copyright 1989 by the Zen Center (p.85). All used by permission of Bantam Books, a division of Bantam Doubleday Dell Publishing Group, Inc.

British Museum Press: *Living Buddhism* by Andrew Powell (p.86).

Buddhist Publication Society Inc.: *A Comprehensive Manual of Abhidharma*, trans. and edited by Mahathera Narada (pp.82–3); *The Life of the Buddha* by Bhikku Nanamoli (pp.30, 32, 43); *Living Buddhist Masters* by Jack Kornfield (p.89); *The Udana*, trans. by John D. Ireland (p.45).

Bruno Cassirer: *Buddhist Scriptures*, trans. and edited by Edward Conze (p.35); *Buddhist Texts through the Ages*, trans. and edited by Edward Conze (pp.42, 48, 50, 101); all by permission of Mrs. Muriel Conze.

Columbia University Press: *Sources of Japanese Tradition*, William Theodore de Bary (ed.) (p.39).

Curzon Press: *The Sutta Nipata* by Saddhatissa (p.33).

Dharma Publishing: *Crystal Mirror* by Tarthang Tulku (pp.26, 64, 65); *Elegant Sayings* by Nagarjuna and Sakya Pandita (pp.24, 48, 91, 104); *The Life and Liberation of Padmasambhava*, trans. by Kenneth Douglas and Gwendolyn Bays (p.47); *Mother of Knowledge* by Namkhai Nyingpo, trans. by Tarthang Tulku (pp.51, 69, 76, 77, 99).

Element Books: *Blessing Power of the Buddhas* by Norma Levine (p.99).

Gaia House: *Fire Dance and Other Poems* by Christopher Titmuss (p.81).

Thich Nhat Hanh: *Old Path, White Clouds* (US/Canadian rights) (p.109).

Library of Tibetan Works and Archives: *Generous Wisdom* (p.29); *A Guide to the Bodhisattva's Way of Life* by Shantideva, trans. by Stephen Batchelor (pp.17, 44–5).

Luzac: *The Elder's Verses: Theragatha and Therigatha*, trans. by K.R. Norman (pp.21, 108).

Manjushri Mahayana Buddhist Centre: *Offering to the Spiritual Guide* by Panchen Losang Chokyi Gyaltsan, trans. by Geshe Kelsang Gyatso (p.17); *Praise of Dependent Relationship* by Je Tsongkhapa, trans. by Geshe Kelsang Gyatso (p.112); both published by Tharpa Publications.

North Atlantic Books: *Morning Dewdrops of the Mind* by Shodo Harada Roshi©1993 by Shodo Harada Roshi (p.21). Reprinted by arrangement with Frog Ltd., c/o North Atlantic Books, PO Box 12327, Berkeley, CA 94712.

Oxford University Press: *The Life and Teaching of Naropa*, trans. by Herbert Guenther,©Oxford University Press 1963 (pp.25, 76, 107), by permission of Oxford University Press.

Pali Text Society: *The Expositor*, edited by Mrs. Rhys Davids, trans. by Pe Maung Tin (p.82); *Samyutta Nikaya*, edited by L. Freer (pp.24, 57).

Parallax Press: reprinted from *Dharma Gaia: A Harvest of Essays in Buddhism and Ecology*, edited by Allan Hunt Badiner, 1990 (pp.50, 85); reprinted from *The Sun My Heart* by Thich Nhat Hanh, 1988 (pp.21, 31, 49); all with permission of Parallax Press, Berkeley, California.

Primary Point Press: *Thousand Peaks* by Mu Soeng Sunim (p.38).

Princeton University Press: *Passionate Enlightenment* by Miranda Shaw,©1994 (pp.22, 76). Reprinted by permission of Princeton University Press.

Rider (Random House): *Ch'an and Zen Teaching* by Lu K'uan Yu (p.86); *Old Path, White Clouds* by Thich Nhat Hanh (world rights XCUSA) (p.109); *A Path with Heart* by Jack Kornfield

world rights XCUSA) (p.33); *The Transmission of Mind* by Charles Luk (p.74).

Shambhala Publications Inc.: from *Crazy Wisdom* by Chogyam Trungpa (pp.18, 46, 72); *The Experience of Insight* by Joseph Goldstein (pp. 98, 123); from *The Healing Buddha* by Raoul Birnbaum,©1979, 1989 (p.97); from *Glimpses of Abhidharma* by Chogyam Trungpa (p.83); from *The Heart of the Buddha* by Chogyam Trungpa (p.26); from *The Hundred Thousand Songs of Milarepa*, trans. by Garma C.C. Chang (pp.36, 98); from *The Lotus-Born* by Yeshe Tsogyal, rans. by Eric Pema Kunsang,©1993 (p.46); from *Mudra* by Chogyam Trungpa (pp.23, 102, 103); from *The Myth of Freedom* by Chogyam Trungpa (p.73); from *The Rain of Wisdom* by Chogyam Trungpa and Nalanda Translation Committee (p.14); from *Shambhala: The Sacred Path f the Warrior* by Chogyam Trungpa (pp.104–5); from *White Sail* by Thinley Norbu, © 1992 p.14); from *The Vimalakirti Nirdesa Sutra* (p.16); from *A Visionary Journey* by Longchenpa, rans. and annotated by Herbert V. Guenther,©1989 (p.71); all reprinted by arrangement with Shambhala Publications Inc., 300 Massachusetts Avenue, Boston, MA 02115.

His Eminence Tai Situpa: Poem in honor of the birth of the Seventeenth Karmapa written for his publication (p.59).

Snow Lion Publications: *Buddha Mind* by Tulku Tondup (p.113); *Selected Works of the Dalai Lama VII: Songs of Spiritual Change*, trans. by Glenn H. Mullin (pp.19, 70–1, 74, 80); Geshe Wangyal quoted in *The Jewelled Staircase* (p.57) .

Theosophical Publishing House: *A Still Forest Pool*, compiled and edited by Jack Kornfield and Paul Breiter (pp.27, 75, 115); *Mother of the Buddhas* by Lex Hixon (p.43); *Noble Theosophists Speak to Theosophists and to the World* (p.117).

Tiwari's Pilgrims Book House, Kathmandu: *Oracles and Demons of Tibet* by Nebesky-Wojkowitz p.105).

Weatherhill: *Zen Mind, Beginner's Mind* by Suzuki Shunruyu (pp.27, 54, 80).

White Pine Press: "Singing Image of An Echo" and "Singing Image of Foam" by Kukai (Kobo Daishi), from *Tantric Poetry of Kukai (Kobo Daishi), Japan's Buddhist Saint*, trans. by Morgan Gibson & Hiroshi Murakami (p.37). Copyright 1982, 1987 by White Pine Press. Reprinted by permission of White Pine Press, Fredonia, NY 14063.

Wisdom Publications: *Drinking the Mountain Stream*,©Brian Cutillo and Lama Kunga Thartse Rinpoche 1995 (p.102); *Heartwood of the Bodhi Tree* by Achaan Buddhadasa, edited by Santikaro Bhikku,©Evolution Liberation 1994 (p.63); *In Praise of Tara*, selected, trans. and introduced by Martin Willson,©Martin Willson 1986 (p.22); *The Middle Length Discourses of the Buddha: A New Translation of the Majjhima Nikaya*, original translation by Bhikku Nanamoli, translation dited and revised by Bhikku Bodhi,©Bhikku Bodhi 1995 (pp.16, 28, 33, 56); *Mind Science: An East–West Dialogue*, by His Holiness the Dalai Lama et al, edited by Daniel Goleman and Robert Thurman,©Mind/Body Medical Institute Inc. & Tibet House, New York, Inc. 1991 p.61); all with permission of Wisdom Publications, 361 Newbury Street, Boston, MA.

Special thanks to Dr. Gyurme Dorje, Wisdom Books, London.

Every effort has been made to find the copyright owners of the material used. However there are a few quotations that have been impossible to trace, and we would be glad to hear from the copyright owners of these quotations so that acknowledgment can be made in any future edition.

The publishers wish to thank the following for the use of pictures:
BRIDGEMAN ART LIBRARY. FORTEAN PICTURE LIBRARY. MICHAEL HOLFORD PHOTOGRAPHS. HORIZON PHOTOGRAPHIC AGENCY. IMAGE BANK. IMAGES COLOUR LIBARY.

QUEST BOOKS are published by the Theosophical Society in America, Wheaton, Illinois 60189–0270, a branch of a world organization dedicated to the promotion of the unity of humanity and the encouragement of the study of religion, philosophy and science, to the end that we may better understand ourselves and our place in the universe. The Society stands for complete freedom of individual search and belief. For further information about its activities, write or call 1–800–669–1571.

The Theosophical Publishing House is aided by the generous support of the Kern Foundation, a trust dedicated to Theosophical education.